The Scrapbook of My Life
Alfie Deyes

PUBLISHED BY BLINK PUBLISHING
3.25, THE PLAZA,
535 KINGS ROAD,
CHELSEA,
LONDON, SW10 0SZ

WWW.BLINKPUBLISHING.CO.UK

FACEBOOK.COM/BLINKPUBLISHING

TWITTER.COM/BLINKPUBLISHING

PB — 978-1-910536-10-0
TPB — 978-1-910536-94-0
HB — 978-1-910536-92-6
EBOOK — 978-1-910536-93-3

A CIP CATALOGUE OF THIS BOOK IS AVAILABLE FROM THE BRITISH LIBRARY.

DESIGN BY BLINK PUBLISHING

PRINTED AND BOUND IN GERMANY

1 3 5 7 9 10 8 6 4 2

PAPERS USED BY BLINK PUBLISHING ARE NATURAL, RECYCLABLE PRODUCTS MADE FROM WOOD GROWN IN
SUSTAINABLE FORESTS. THE MANUFACTURING PROCESSES CONFORM TO THE ENVIRONMENTAL REGULATIONS
OF THE COUNTRY OF ORIGIN.

BLINK PUBLISHING IS AN IMPRINT OF THE BONNIER PUBLISHING GROUP

WWW.BONNIERPUBLISHING.CO.UK

The Scrapbook of My Life

OF

ALFIE DEYES

BLINK
bringing you closer

The Scrapbook of My Life App
(Coming in April 2016!)

SCAN HERE

Hey guys!

I really hope you enjoy The Scrapbook of My Life, but I don't want this book to be all about me! So I've left the odd page either blank or partly filled so that you can grab a pen and get involved too, and save your memories for you to look back on in the future.

Those who purchased my other books (The Pointless Books) loved the integrated apps! So of course I had to have an app feature in this one too! Just look out for the scannable icons and point your device at them to reveal some never-before-seen content. Including some super-old footage of me as a little kid that I probably shouldn't have put out there for the world to see... but it's too late now!

You can also add your own photos to the memory booth and share them with me, your friends and the rest of #ThePointlessGang! Just don't forget that you need an Internet connection, so that you can download it and use it on your iPhone, iPad or other Android devices.

Enjoy guys!

Alfie x

THE SCRAPBOOK OF MY LIFE

You know that messy/dirty little diary you tuck away under your bed crammed with random ~~mou~~ moments of your life? That's kinda what this is for me! This little book you're ~~holding~~ is packed full of random little stories that have ~~happened~~ to me throughout my life so far.

I'm currently ~~21~~ 22 years old and looking back on my life so far... saying 'so far' sounds stupid. I'm only 22 haha! I'm half writing this for you to read and half for myself to look back on when I'm older and can laugh at all the things I've done in the past.

I don't really know where or how to begin... I'm not used to this writing thing at all! After all, I dropped English language about 5 years ago...

In fact, what I'll do is leave some spaces/pages empty so that you can fill out parts yourself to look back on in the future. It'll kinda be like a shared diary between you and I!

Right, since I still have no idea where to start, I guess my birth is the best place? I thought it'd be best for me to go visit my parents house and dig through the thousands of photos they've taken of me throughout the years. Annnnd also pick both their brains, as they remember EVERYTHING!

Ugh I just realised that I'm going to have to hand-scan in all the early photos of me as there was no such thing as a digital camera when i was a kid! haha

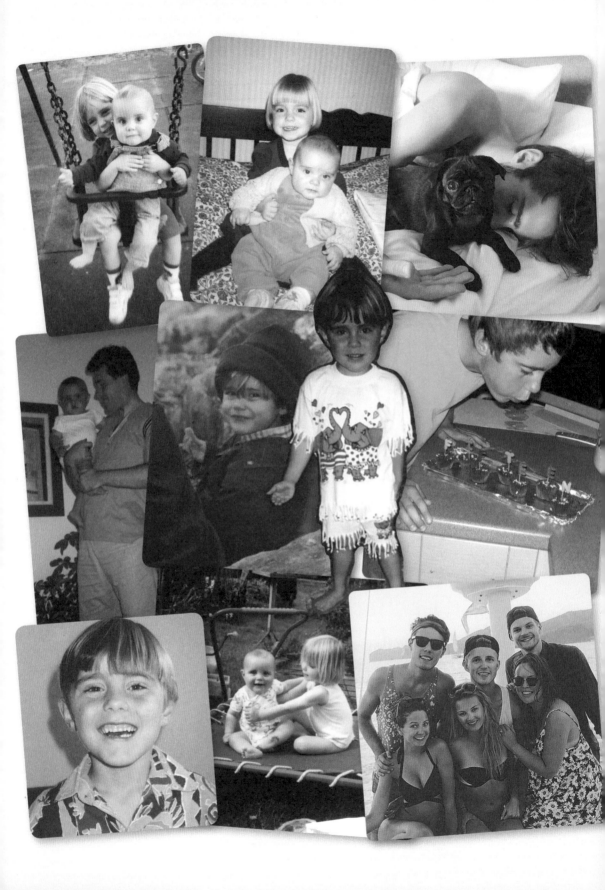

BABY STATS

20 minute birth

9.2lb

Caesarean birth

Asthma

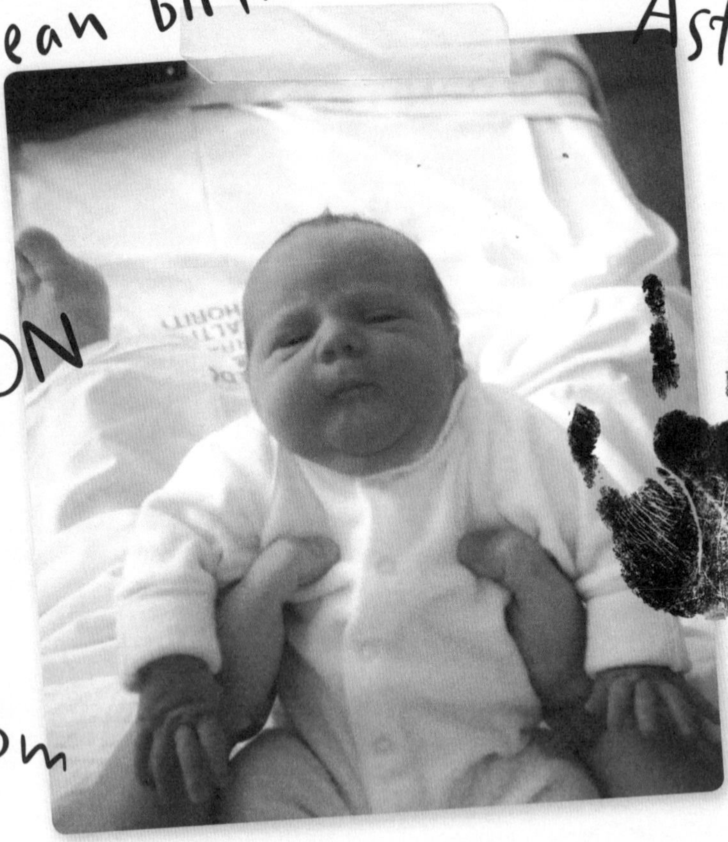

LONDON

3:40pm

Cyst on my lung

17.09.1993

ALFRED SIDNEY DEYES

Shadow on my head

What about you?

Obviously I don't happen to remember being born so I can't exactly write the beginning of this book acting like it was yesterday. But what I do know is that being born is weird. Really weird. Me, I was pulled out of my mum's stomach... nice! I was a big baby at 9.2lb and I'm guessing that most of that was my head.

My sister has always told me the reason I was a caesarean birth was because my head ~~was~~ was so damn big... I kind of believe her!

Usually when you're born you're placed in your mother's arms right away, but for some reason they gave me to my dad and my mum didn't actually get to hold me for about 20 minutes.

The doctors and nurses then found out I had a cyst on my lung, which meant I was in and out of hospital constantly. It eventually went away after 9 months!

Basically I was a very easy baby... NOT!

oh yeah.. another little thing which made me really easy was having baby bronchiolitis for the first 2 ~~years~~ years of my life!

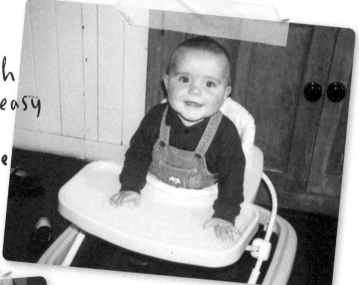

This literally meant I went non-stop in and out of hospital during this time period, ~~mean~~ resulting in many of my baby photos being taken in hospital :·)

13

HOW DID I FORGET TO WRITE DOWN THE STORY EXPLAINING THE BLACK PATCH OF HAIR AT THE FRONT OF MY HEAD?!!

Right stick with me on this one as it's a pretty weird story that I myself don't quite believe, but my mum's friend is sure it happened.

So apparently if a pregnant woman asks you to do something for her and you forget or don't do it, it's bad luck? Yeah that's new to me too!

Anyways, when my mum was pregnant with me, my mum asked her friend if she could pick her up a Cornetto ice cream on her way back and you guessed it... she forgot! My mum's friend was sooo annoyed with herself and kept on saying she had to go back to the shop and buy one for my mum, otherwise her child (me) will be born with a mark somewhere on its body.

Annnd there we have it! I was born with a black patch of hair at the front of my head, which is still there until today! My mum calls it my Cornetto patch haha! This is literally the best example of why mothers know best. I'll never question anything my mum says, she's ALWAYS right!

THINGS I LOVED AS A BABY...

O Dressing up in anything, especially dresses...

O Following my older sister Poppy around
   everywhere. I was literally like her shadow!

O Sleeping with my finger in my dad's ear... Yeah
   I don't even know what to say about this one.
   I've just been told that it was apparently a thing.

O Having my toenails painted.

O Spot the dog!

Climbing over/on/in every single piece
of furniture in the house.

O My dad carrying me everywhere because I refused
   to walk.

here's your page t

16

ll in

LONDON

I was born in London and lived there until I was 3¾ (yep the ¾ is important when you're little) and the only thing I really remember is our amazing garden. My entire family lived within a 5 minute walk of our house, which meant my ~~cute~~ aunts, uncles, grandparents and cousins were over all the time. I loved it! Our garden was pretty big and had a lot of things any child would love!

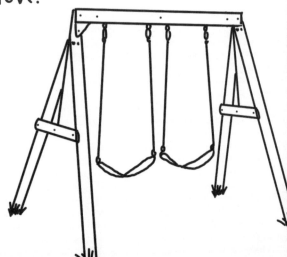

BRIGHTON

Moving to Brighton meant not only moving away from our family and friends, but changing nursery for me and school for my sister.

Only being $3\frac{3}{4}$ at the time, I ~~expect~~ suppose I was a bit too young to realise what was actually going on, but for my parents it was a big deal! But I'm so glad they made that decision because Brighton is my favourite city in the entire world!

MY FAMILY TREE

Grandma — Grandad   Grandma — Grandad

Uncle | Aunt | Uncle | Aunt | Mum — Dad | Aunt | Uncle | Uncle | Uncle | Aunt

Boy | Girl

Boy | Boy

Poppy | Me

Boy | Girl

Boy | Girl

20

your family tree

NURSERY was a lot of FUN

I mean, I swear it's impossible not to enjoy hanging out with all of your friends in one place AND having tons of different toys to **play** with! I loved playing in the sandpit with Morgan & Izzy, **my two nursery besties.**

I **used to** have speech impediment sessions every day because I **mispronounced** certain words, like instead of 'socks', I'd say 'docks'... nice one Alfie!! haha

MY NURSERY MEMORIES

I have so many memories of the time I spent at Balfour Infant school. I swear when you're little you just have no worries in your life... well, you do, but they're like 'Oh no I can't find the right piece of Lego to build my tower'.

To be popular in my class you had to either be good at skipping or cats-cradle and luckily I loved both of those things. I'd spend every break we had **practising with my friends. I mean, I was no expert,** but If I was asked to whip out a little **cross-over-armed-double-skip or the old Eiffel Tower** ~~cats-cradle~~ cats-cradle, I could do it haha!

One very vivid memory I have is a bit of a weird one... Let me start by telling you ~~~~ the ending and then explain myself. I got caught in the

Nice bowl cut, thanks Mum!

reading corner just after punching a friend in the mouth and *knocking* her tooth out!

Okay, okay so this is how it went:

My teacher was showing something to the class when one of my friends (can't remember her name... I was like 4 years old) asked me if I'd sneak off to the reading/book area with her. Now, to be fair, I thought this was just for a bit of fun! We managed to sneak off **without the teacher realising and once we were around the corner tucked** away, my friend **said** 'Alfie can you punch me in the mouth so my wobbly tooth will come out?' Why, I'll never **quite know!**
She could have just pulled it out like a normal person.

Anyways for some reason at the time I thought it was a damn fun idea and then punched her...
INSTANTLY she began to cry and the teacher came running over to ask me what was going on..! Well, let's just say that was a tricky one to explain, as my friend sat there with her tooth in her hand, crying, with blood dripping out of her mouth.

School name

Teacher's name

Favourite school dinners

School play memory

MY MUM!

My mum's a super-creative person and always put so much time and **effort into activities for Poppy and I.** Everyday we'd be doing something new and fun like painting in the garden, decorating our clothes or even **building a stage for us to perform on!** Annnnd this stage has **resulted in multiple videos of me dancing** in dresses... I'm not even going to try and explain myself. It is what it is!

We used to love painting in the garden...

It was a few days before my friend Morgan's 4th birthday, so mum and I set out to buy him a present. We popped round to a little shop not far from our house that sold birthday decorations and little gifts for parties. After spending a good 10 minutes searching for the perfect present, the only thing I managed to find was a ~~funny~~ funny birthday card... but that wasn't really going to cut it haha! I couldn't NOT give him a present!

Whilst waiting for mum to pay for the card, I spotted it! The perfect present! Next to me, sitting ~~—————~~ in a barrel full of soft toys, staring up at me was a little brown teddy. I popped it up on the counter. Morgan's birthday present was sorted!!... Well, at least I thought it was.

Mum was about to start wrapping up the teddy because if I attempted it myself... well, it would have looked like a four-year-old had wrapped it...

I remember taking the little floppy teddy out of the shopping bag and passing him to mum. And that's where it kinda went downhill. I mean, he was just too soft and cool... aannnd basically long story short... I kept **him hahaha! Which left Morgan yet again with no birthday** present!! So the following day we had to pop out and I ended **up buying him a pillow. What a great present** Alfie...a pillow!

He did have eyes but they've fallen out over the years...

To this day if Morgan ever comes over my house and happens to see Floppy, he tries to steal him back off of me

Write your favourite story about your friends...

STARTING "REAL" SCHOOL

After having so much fun at Balfour Infant School, it was time for me to move on up in the world and start year 3! I remember at the time feeling really odd about this. One ~~minute~~ minute you're one of the oldest children in your entire school, then literally a few weeks later, after the summer holidays, you start your new school and you're the youngest and smallest you can possibly be! Weird!

For some reason I have a few school memories that stick in my head more than any others... they're not even particularly amazing... well actually one of them is pretty cool so I'll tell you that one!

I was never a packed lunch kid, instead I preferred to eat hot meals for lunch which meant my parents gave me something like £1.80 each day to get a meal from the school canteen. Usually I'd be given a £1, a 50p and a few 10p coins or something, but I remember one day in particular my mum and dad left me a £2 for lunch. I spent the entire day playing with it in my pocket, flicking it up in the air, trying to guess which side it'd land on and rolling it across the table to and from each hand and then it happened! I kid you not, like this sounds stupid, but it's true!! **The middle part** separated from the coin, I'm not even joking! It split into the silver middle and the golden-coloured outside! I was obsessed! ...well kinda... until it came to lunchtime and I was so ~~hungry~~ hungry that I had no choice but to spend it on my school meal. Without sounding stupid, I've literally regretted it to this day!

SCAN HERE

Every single time I get a £2 I ALWAYS check to see if I can push the middle out ...and not once has it happened again!

MY FIRST PROPER HOBBY

I remember having to slip on my little black plimsoles, white T-shirt and shorts to play silly games in the school hall and somehow it counted as PE... we literally spent an hour throwing balls to each other and running around cones... why was that even a thing?

But gymnastics was different! I'd never taken part in any gymnastics before Mrs Caines began teaching my class. I mean I'd always loved running around and jumping off of ~~trees~~ things like walls and between my sofas (even though mum wasn't so keen), but never thought of taking gymnastics lessons. Well that was until I met Mrs Caines. I think she could just tell how much fun I had in her lessons and for some reason thought I was pretty good, so pushed me a lot harder than the other children in my class. If they were learning how to do a cartwheel, I was learning how to do a handstand.

It wasn't because I asked to do more difficult manoeuvres, Mrs Caines just encouraged me to do them. She believed in me and wanted me to succeed!

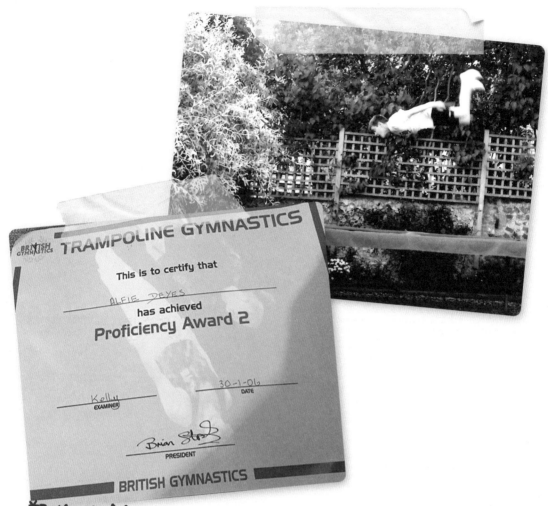

TRAMPOLINE GYMNASTICS

BRITISH GYMNASTICS

This is to certify that

ALFIE DEYES

has achieved

Proficiency Award 2

Kelly
EXAMINER

30-1-06
DATE

Brian St
PRESIDENT

BRITISH GYMNASTICS

I think Mrs Caines played an important part in who I am today. Although she may not realise this and might not even remember teaching me haha! Having her show me that if I put my mind to learning these basic moves, I could improve and learn things I never thought I could... I honestly think the courage and belief in myself she stamped on me has stuck with me to this very day and I'm so thankful for everything she taught me

HaHaa I DON'T EVEN KNOW WHERE TO START EXPLAINING THIS MEMORY...

So I'll start again with what happened and then try my best to somehow explain why **I did what I did!**

I SHAVED MY DAD'S HEAD WHILST HE WAS SLEEPING!

I have no idea why I did it, I was too young at the time to remember... So what I'll do is explain what I think happened from what my parents have **told me over the years. My dad went to sleep just** like every other night and so did I. At some point during the night I got up (whether I was asleep or not while I did all of this no one will ever know), went into **their bedroom, picked up his little beard trimmer and shaved a spiral shape into the back of his head without** him waking up... I can't imagine my dad looked too great at work the next day with his suit on and new 'hair cut' haha!

I probably shouldn't have done this.

POPULAR CRAZES AT MY SCHOOL

I became OBSESSED with any craze! I couldn't just be average or okay at anything, I had to be amazing! Not to be better than anyone else, but to show myself that if I put the time into whatever it was, I could succeed!

This started out with Pokémon cards. I would beg my dad to buy me packs every weekend. I'd do extra jobs around the house to earn little bits of money to save up to buy packs. You name it, I'd do it. It was the unknown that I loved. The risk you took with spending hard-earned money hoping that you'd open the packet to find a rare card to take into school the next day. Then I discovered the Diablo... it took over my life. You didn't need money to get better, you just needed skill. For me, time = skill.

I would spend literally every second I wasn't in the classroom practising little tricks like over my leg, around my neck and the good old Chinese whip! (That was one of my best).

The Diablo became SO popular in my school, the teachers arranged for a local circus shop to come in one day and host a competition to find out who the best was from each year group (I was in year 5). I knew

I had a pretty good chance, but also knew that my friends Max and Asa were pretty good too.

After many tedious rounds of basic little tricks, I secured my place in the final 3... the final 3 being myself, Max and Asa haha! I can't quite remember how or why, but Asa went out next leaving myself and Max!! The pressure was on! All those hours spent practising were about to be made worthwhile!

Out of nowhere Max suddenly drops his Diablo off the string, something that would send him out of the competition, but no... it bounces off of the assembly hall floor and lands back on his string...no one except me notices! Do I tell the judge what happened and place 1st, or keep it between myself and Max?!

I decided not to tell anyone and ended up placing 2nd with Max winning!! And from that day forward, Max and I have always joked about who's better and who should have actually won!

Next was the yo-yo, but I'm not even going to go into that one! I basically spent another bajillion hours learning random little tricks haha!

DO MORE OF WHAT WHAT Makes YOU HAPPY

CHRISTMas iS THE BEST TIME OF YEaR!

Everyone was happy, there was lots of delicious food and, little did I know, there were also TWO kittens coming! Poppy and I had sleepovers every Christmas Eve which usually meant me sleeping in Poppy's room on a mattress on the floor. My room was only about 10m away, but we always shared a room because it meant whoever woke up first could wake the other up and we'd both get to open our presents earlier!

After ~~running~~ running and dragging our heavy stockings into

Mum and Dad's room, jumping on their bed and making them both get out of bed, it was time to head downstairs and open our presents. I'm not sure what your Christmas traditions are like (if you celebrate Christmas) but we have always opened our stockings (from Santa) on Mum and Dad's bed... no earlier than 7am! And then we all meet downstairs in our pyjamas for some breakfast in the front room.

It happened whilst opening all of our presents to and from each other. Dad snuck off to another room to get one of Poppy's gifts... which was odd since I couldn't understand why it wasn't under the tree with everyone else's presents. As Poppy opened the loosely wrapped box, two tiny little ginger kittens came bouncing out!! My sister, being the stroppy little girl she often was, started crying and ran upstairs because she 'didn't want kittens for Christmas'... What even?

Now, what I'm about to say sounds like some kind of film scene, but honestly it did happen!! Both the little kittens followed Poppy upstairs and sat outside the toilet door whilst Pop sat inside crying!

I think that was the moment Poppy fell in love with them and realised Todd and Tilly were the best Christmas present ever!

For ages the two kittens were called Todd and Tim, but after taking him to the vets we found out that Tim was in fact a girl and so we chan changed her name to Tilly! Toddler (Todd) and Tilly!!

My favourite time of year

Always DO SOMETHING UNTIL YOU CAN DO IT. Don't Quit

SCAN HERE

CAMPING

Camping trips with my family were just the best! We used to FILL up the car with everything we could possibly want to take with us! Even double duvets instead of sleeping bags so that it was more comfortable. And the most fun bit of all was that it wasn't just our family, but our friends' families too! Every year we'd go in a big group of about 6 families... Having water fights during the day, going on long bike rides and making camp fires in the evening to roast marshmallows on!

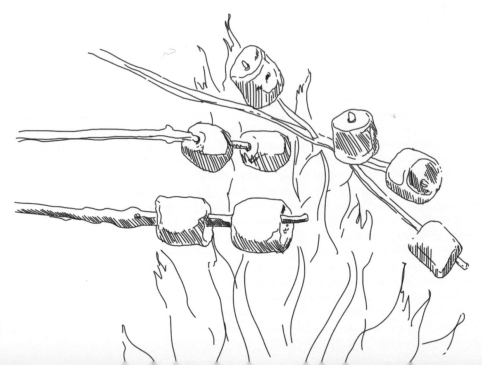

STARTING ANYTHING NEW IS SCARY...

Let alone separating from half of your friends to start an entirely new school with new subjects, new teachers and new pupils... buuut everyone has to do it!

Dressed in my new uniform and feeling like a grown up, I was soo excited to start secondary school and meet new people. I remember my first lesson with everyone sitting in their little groups of friends and not really talking to people they **didn't already know haha!**

Little did I know this very day I'd be meeting some of my best and oldest friends for the very **first time.**

I was that kid in your class who got dropped off and picked up by his mum everyday... Usually this would be embarrassing, but it meant I got to wake up 20 minutes later every morning! In fact, I'd even get my mum to **pick up my friends on the way so** they didn't have to walk either!

*If you haven't already gathered, my parents are **the best parents in the world***

I think it was also a tiny bit easier for me, as Poppy was three years above me in school so for the first two years of secondary school, I knew she was there if I ever needed anything. In one of the first few weeks my English teacher tried to give me a ~~20~~ 30 minute detention for not doing my homework. Buuuut I had a legit reason for it not getting done (I can't quite remember exactly what that reason was, but it was a good one... even if it was or wasn't true).

I remember saying I needed the toilet, calling Poppy up and asking her to come down to the English section and persuade my teacher not to give me a detention!! It worked haha!!

$$a^2 + b^2 = c^2$$

I always enjoyed school and always wanted to learn. I wouldn't say I was crazy smart, but If I was interested in a subject and wanted to do well I'd always get good marks. But when it came down to subjects that didn't really interest me, I'd always revise just enough to pass so that I could put the rest of my time into the subjects I enjoyed e.g. maths and science.

My family call me

'GOLDEN BOY'

I have no idea when this first started but it's stuck since such a young age. I'm guessing it's because I've always had a ~~nack~~ knack for talking my way out of things/getting away with stuff I should get told off for. It's kinda hard to explain haha! Basically if I were to get away with something and Poppy didn't, she'll say it's because I'm 'the golden child' or 'golden boy' and my parents' favourite. Whiiichhh obviously isn't true as no parent has a favourite child. But it's funny because so often I'll get away with doing something that Poppy would <u>never</u> get away with!

Over the years it's become more and more silly and and if I were to ever go for lunch with one of my parents or clothes shopping or anything where Poppy isn't with us, it's because I'm 'golden boy' haha!

4TH PLACE... OUT OF 4!

I'd never had a gymnastics competition before so I didn't quite know what to expect. I had learnt my floor routine inside out and how to do one of those funny arm-up-in-the-air things that you have to do to the judges at the beginning of your routine. As Mum and I **watched people of other age groups take their turns, we realised that** I was the only person wearing a vest and shorts... literally no one else except me! I **looked at my coach, embarrassed...** Mum went to ask a member of staff if I could buy a ~~new~~ leotard at the venue and luckily for me, I could! I ran over to the little shop area and picked up a plain black leotard and popped it on. **SO MUCH BETTER!** I suddenly looked like I had a chance haha.

Every gym floor feels different, some can be more springy than others so I was a bit unsure of what to expect. I walked over to the centre of the floor, did the arm thingy followed by my routine (which actually went pretty well). **Next was my vault, which** again can vary vastly due to the equipment used on the day, but luckily for me it managed to go okay. They began to call out the names in order of positions from 4th – 1st, which started with mine! Meaning I came 4th!! I was happy **with that,** considering it was my very first competition!

Oh yeahhhh... I should probably let you know that in my group there were four of us.. HAHA! Buuuut 4th is 4th and that's all people who weren't there on the day needed to know ha!

Tons of training went by and it was time for the Sussex boys finals. This was a _lot_ bigger, more prestigious and difficult than my original 4th placing competition.

The age group was 11-13 and I'd only just turned 11... not exactly fair considering all the other boys were either 12 or 13. Annnd the boy who'd won the two previous years in a row was 13 years old and up against me....! As we warmed up I kept myself to myself and didn't really speak to any of the other boys. They were all a lot louder — talking about previous wins and moves they'd learnt for their routines. Safe to say I was pooing my pants! I did my very best and just like last time everything seemed to go ~~sooooote~~ pretty well. One of the straight-faced judges even cracked a little smirk!
A few hours later, after watching the other groups do their part, it was time for the medal ceremony! Each category sat in a line and were called up in front of everyone, one at a time. 'Sussex boys 11-13 floor and vault'... I literally felt like staying sat down I was so nervous.

They started with 3rd place... my name wasn't called. The boy, who'd won both years previously, stood next to me, whispered in my ear 'I bet I've won again'. I looked at him in disbelief as they called HIS NAME out!! As it hit him and his face dropped I whispered back 'no you didn't haha'. At this point I didn't even care who'd won, I was just so happy that he didn't!

'ALFIE DEYES'

I looked around confused... wait huh! I'd won!! As I walked up and took my place on the highest podium I looked down and smirked at the boy stood next to me holding his silver medal! I'll never forget that moment!

what
did you
win?

THE TIME I SHAVED MY HAIR FOR CHARITY

My school was having a charity day where everyone could wear what they wanted if they donated 50p to charity. There were also lots of fun activities they could get involved in instead of lessons for small amounts of money (which also went to charity) e.g. throw a wet sponge at ~~the~~ the principal's head... play in a football tournament for the afternoon... or buy cupcakes from students who were having a cake sale. But, me being me, I thought I'd take it to the next level! So a few weeks before the charity day, I decided I'd shave my side-fringed-Justin-Bieber-style hair completely off and ask friends and family to donate money for me doing so!

The evening before the school charity day I went down to where I usually got my haircut and asked them to completely shave it off! I explained the reasons behind the bald head and my hairdresser agreed to do the cut for free as it was for a good cause. He said he'd start at the back of my head so that I couldn't see how short it was and if I did decide to change my mind, it would be too late as, by the time I'd see it, the entire back of my head would be hairless haha! I ~~cannot~~ remember seeing **my mum's face...** literally like this Ö

I mean, I knew it was going to be short, but mannn it was SHORT! Literally bald!! I'd never seen my actual **head bald before** – it was sooo weird. **I remember getting home and cry**ing so much because I hated how I looked! I couldn't look in the mirror without wanting to go back in time. The only thing that kept me happy was knowing that I'd raised **a lot of money for young people between the ages of 11-18 who were terminally ill. My first bald day at school was hard!**

Sooo many of my friends had donated money to me for shaving my head and wanted to see what it looked like and the last thing I wanted to do was show people my bald head, **which I was still not used to! I remember wearing a hat as much as I could to hide my hairless** head. But thinking back to it, I shouldn't have been embarrassed at all! Not many young boys would completely shave their hair off to raise money for charity!

I'm soo glad I stuck with the idea and did it!

I'M NOT a CHEAT.

Well I'm not 'usually' a cheat.

What I mean is that I'm good at cheating and I never get caught... except this one time haha!

Monopoly has always been one of my favourite games! I think it's because it's silly and fun, but also a little bit strategic and I love coming up with strategies to solve problems. And in Monopoly terms, that's either not having enough money to buy something or trying to persuade another player to trade a card I need.

Well anyways, this time, let's just say money wasn't the issue... I had PLENTY of that! So, as per all Monopoly games, we played for hours and hours with people gradually becoming bankrupt and leaving the game to watch TV, play Snake on their phones or to grab snacks from the fridge. Now I honestly can't remember who won the game, but strangely that's not the important bit in this story.

I woke up the next day with a text from my friend Neil asking me to pop over as he had something to show me (this is the boy whose house we played Monopoly at the previous night). Neil only lived on the road next to me, so later on in the day I ran over and letsss just say I wasn't expecting him to show me what he did!! Is recording a friendly Monopoly game on a camcorder a normal thing? I suppose... Neil's Dad had just bought a new camera and was playing around with it that evening.

With his entire family huddled around his computer screen, I pull up a chair and sit-down. He clicks play... I still have no idea what's happening at this point! Everyone around me starts to laugh as we all sit watching as I 'get up to go to the toilet' whilst playing the game, walk past the Banker (person who looks after all of the money in the game) and grab a wad of money whilst no one is watching...
I leave the room and return a few minutes later and continue playing as if nothing had happened.

GO TO
JAIL

I LITERALLY GOT CAUGHT STEALING MONOPOLY MONEY ON CAMERAAAA! Hahaa! I swear I don't always cheat, it was just that once...

RUNESCAPE AND HALO... TWO ONLINE GAMES THAT I PLAYED FOR SOOO MANY HOURS EACH AND EVERY DAY!

It sounds weird, but when playing these games it felt like I was in a zone. I can't quite describe it, but time would pass like crazy! I remember once my friend came over at lunchtime, us both grabbing snacks and sitting at my family computer to play RuneScape. Next thing I knew, my parents came upstairs and asked if my friend was staying over? We both turned and were like... huh? Why are you asking that, not realising it was 11pm! We literally hadn't stopped playing for 8 hours!! (My Mum's just read this page and said she wouldn't let me game this long but I definitely did!)

I'd spend entire weekends with 8-12 friends all crammed into one bedroom, each with our own Xbox and TV brought over by our parents early on a Friday night. We'd then spend all of Friday evening, all of Saturday and most of Sunday (until going home in the evening) playing Halo 2.

We'd all be running on literally a few hours sleep with our eyes STUCK to the screens. If anyone were to fall asleep, they'd for sure be pranked by everyone else, so I'd always make sure that I'd stay awake the entire time haha. And that took a LOT of fizzy drinks, pizzas and chocolate..!
I can't even describe how fun these weekends were! Hanging out with so many friends at once and gaming all day/all night.

START LIVING doing & Things you ENJOY

I was given pocket money for doing chores around the house... **well,** that was until I realised that I could earn the same amount of money much faster by doing easier/more fun things than cleaning and hoovering or drying the dishes. This started off at a really young **age and gradually** became more and more apparent as I got older. I'd like to say **selling cards** outside my house was my very first job at the age of **around 7 or 8 haha!**

I used to fold a **piece of A4 paper from my parents'** printer and write 'Happy Birthday' on it. **Or if I was feeling particularly fancy,** I'd walk down the road and look out for a nice-looking flower, pick it and stick it to the front of the card. I'd then **take a small table and chair, and** place these outside the front of my house and wait for generous-looking people to walk past. These people weren't yet aware that they needed a card for a family member/friend, **but it didn't take much** ~~persuasion~~ persuasion **to make them part with 50p or £1** when a smiling child is asking them to purchase a handmade card haha!

I used to do a lot of little things like that and over the years they evolved and changed into other things, **such as** doing my **sister's chores if** she didn't want to do them so that I got double the pocket **money that week.**

And then came 'my' paper round...
One of the first jobs a lot of teenagers get in the UK is a paper round, which is basically delivering newspapers either early in the morning (no chance I'd ever wake up that early) or in the evening (my newspapers had to be delivered before 6pm). You have to be 14 or older to get a job as a paper boy/girl... but as usual I came up with a scheme to get the job whilst being 13.

I asked my friend's brother, who was 16 at the time, to apply for the job and then he let me pick up the papers each day and paid me the money at the end of each week! I probably wouldn't do this if I were you... thinking back to it he could have easily taken a percentage of the money and never told me! I'm pretty sure he didn't... and if he did, it serves me right haha!

As you can tell by now, growing up I always did what I could to make money in the most beneficial way possible for me and it kinda didn't stop with my paper round! This is going to make me sound so lazy, but I see it more as finding a good solution to something I didn't want to do. And in this case, that was to go out in the cold for 20 minutes every day (minus Sunday), delivering newspapers to houses (even though it was my job). **I knew my dad** liked going on early morning walks, so he used to deliver **my papers every Saturday** for me whilst walking to the local shop to buy a paper for himself **(thanks Dad!!)**. This left me with **Monday to Friday. Except it kinda didn't** because the majority of the time I'd leave it so late on purpose that my mum used to end up driving me around stopping at each door *whilst I* ran out of the car and popped the paper through the letterbox, jumped back in and repeated for the 37 houses I delivered to. Looking back I don't know why Mum **didn't just tell me to quit the job haha!** Mum and Dad collectively did the majority of the work!

This **happened** ~~unless~~ **unless for some reason Mum couldn't**

help me out and it wasn't a Saturday. In this case, I worked out the quickest route, timed it on foot, skateboard, scooter and bike. Turns out using a scooter was the quickest, **so I used to be able to scooter the** entire round in just over 12 minutes... don't ask me how I remember that haha!

UGH I remember a few *times having* to **deliver them in the morning as I was busy after school and literally walking into** spiders webs outside every single front door! Then trying to get the web off of my face with my hand and rubbing newspaper ink all over my face... **great!!**

My worst/dream job...

You know what's the best? Spending time with your family! Growing up I used to go on holiday once a year to places like Greece, Turkey and Portugal. We'd stay in pretty basic accommodation, but this didn't matter because the best part of the holidays were spending time **with my family sunbathing, messing about in the sea and exploring.**

Back in 2005 to 2006 we stayed right on the beach in a little town clalled Yalicavak, Turkey for a week.

It was a super-friendly little town with a row of local shops and stalls around the corner, which Poppy and I would visit a few times a day buying random little things we'd never actually use like the metal drum I **bought myself** or the laser pen I BEGGED Mum and Dad to let me buy for days and days...haha! We never used them, buuut at the time they were amazing. We'd spend all day swimming in the pool/sea and running back and **forth from the little ice cream ~~stall~~ shop buying Magnums (my favourite ice cream).**

I remember buying a little fishing rod with Dad and walking around for ages to find a little jetty that we could fish off and we actually caught a fish! Not even joking! We enjoyed this holiday so much we went back the following two years!

My favourite holiday has been...

I'M NOT REALLY QUITE SURE HOW ANY OF THIS HAPPENED, OR WHY IT HAPPENED TO ME... BUT IT DID.

My school had a school council (a school council is a representative group of students who have been proposed and elected by their peers to represent their views and raise issues with the Senior Managers and Governors of their school.)
Yes I did just copy that down from Google...

Anyways! Thinking back, I'm not really sure how I ended up being in the school council, nor am I sure how I ended up being Vice Deputy Head of my house... but I was! In simple terms, it meant I had to attend one meeting every few months and chat about ways we could improve certain things about the school e.g. the uniform (I'll come to that one in a sec), litter issues and how the teachers can make the pupils more engaged in lesson time. My favourite part was that we got to miss out on lessons for the meeting, and have tea and biscuits!

Somehow my involvement in the school council lead to me being voted for the Vice Chair for South East of England's student council – which meant not representing my friends anymore, but representing the SOUTH EAST of England!! I'd occasionally get to miss a day of school and get driven to a super-posh school a few hours away to chat about what my school is doing to make it the best it possibly can be for its pupils. And yep – you guessed it – drink more tea or hot chocolate and eat more biscuits.

ALFIE DEYES
Vice Chair for South East of England's Student Council

I'm not going to bother sitting here and write much more about all of these weird school council opportunities/moments I had, but I just wanna jot down one more before I forget!! When I was in Year 10, my Head Teacher decided to move to a new school, which meant we needed to find a new one to replace him.

Now, usually this would be nothing to do with the pupils... but again like with all these other little stories, for some weird reason, I was involved. I spent the day interviewing possible Head Teachers and jotting down what I liked and didn't like about them; literally things like how friendly they were, how they sat, if they were too formal, if they were funny! I was one of five opinions in the final decision!! And, in case you were wondering, yep I did vote for the one who got picked in the end!

Ooh wait! Another ~~quick~~ quick story, as it's funny I promise!

Towards the end of Year 10, when the new Head Teacher started working at our school, he decided he wanted us to refresh the uniform and asked me what I thought it should be like. So I decided it should be a super-strict blazer and tie for Years 7-9 and then much more casual with a white T-shirt and black jeans for years 10-11... and they went for it!!!

I literally made it so my Year (10) and the Year I was about to go into didn't really have to wear uniform, but the rest of the school did and got away with it!!

Vice Captains

Alfie Deyes 11STM
Tilly Grivell 11STM

EVENINGS AFTER SCHOOL...

I'm not quite sure what it is about drama and acting that I love so much, I think it may be the buzz that you get once you walk off stage. Actually I think it's also about the friendships that you make with all the cast and crew putting on the show. You'd spend sooo many hours with the team each day and it feels kinda like your new family!

During school I was in three musicals:

Fiddler on the Roof

West Side Story

Jesus Christ Superstar

As soon as it hit 3:15pm, my friends and I would all head down to our local park (usually Blakers or Preston) and just hang out. Not in a dodgy-looking-teenage-mob way — we'd just relax in the sun, kick a football around, eat snacks and chat for hours and hours.

I've always had just as many female friends as male. I don't really understand the 'you can't be friends with a girl without fancying them' thing... I'd spend time with girls in the exact same way I would with boys. Being so close to Poppy while growing up probably influenced my respectful attitude towards girls.

IT WAS GREAT FUN BEING PART OF SOMETHING AFTER SCHOOL.

PLANNING & SETTING Goals IS key

NO ONE ELSE IN SCHOOL WATCHED YouTube LIKE MY FRIENDS AND ME...

We didn't visit the site to watch dogs riding skateboards or cats falling off walls... well, occasionally we did, but mostly we watched 'YouTubers' – people who uploaded videos frequently to their own little pages on the site. There weren't that many 'YouTubers' around at the time, so there wasn't much variety if you liked that kind of thing.

I think the reason I became so obsessed with watching these 'YouTubers' was because they were being themselves! They weren't acting, they weren't even reading a script; they were just chatting about topics that interested them or filming what they got up to that day. It felt like such a refreshing change from scripted TV shows with unrealistic storylines. But, more than that, you knew that the person you were watching behind the camera was just like you! A normal person! But they just happened to be on the other side of a computer screen.

My friends and I had always filmed stupid little videos when hanging out playing basketball, doing tricks on the trampoline and skateboarding. So instead of the videos being held on a memory stick, we began to put them on YouTube. We **didn't** aim to gain lots of views or subscribers; it was just somewhere we could put them so that we could all watch them whenever we liked.

After putting up a few of the most embarrassing skateboarding/parkour videos, I began to edit videos of myself playing video games (such as Halo 2 and 3, and Modern Warfare 2). I didn't have any experience in filming or editing, but since I was making the videos purely for fun, *I also didn't have the pressure* of having to create them in a certain way to get a good grade in an exam. So I suppose I just spent all my spare time after school learning how to film and edit the best I could... and to do this I watched sooo many editing tutorials on ~~YouTube~~ YouTube of course!

I remained obsessed with watching YouTubers, even while I made my own gaming videos! I begged my dad to take me to London to see CharlieIsSoCoolLike (one of the first YouTubers I became obsessed with) perform live. It was a ~~~~ pretty weird thing to spend my time watching someone else sit in their room chatting about funny topics, so persuading my dad that it was a good idea to travel all the way to London to see him (and not even meet him) was pretty hard ha!

I managed to persuade Dad though, and after hours of queuing up in line I got to see CharlieIsSoCoolLike live and it was awesome! It was strange seeing someone in person, who I'd watched for so long every week, literally standing there in front of me!!

Going to this event made me even more obsessed with YouTube and made me want to start making videos of myself (even more) than I ever had before!

I remember sitting down and making my very first YouTube video like it was yesterday. Balancing the family camera on a stack of Xbox games and DVDs (adjusting the stack a little so the camera was at head height), I pressed the record button without knowing what I was going to talk about or how I was even going to introduce myself...

'Hello! Hey! Hey guys! Helloooo, how're you doing? Hello, my name's Alfie!'

It literally took me about 1,000 takes JUST to say hello to the camera! Not to mention ~~much~~ how quietly I was speaking

MY OLD VIDEOS...

since I didn't want my family to overhear me talking to myself (the camera). I didn't want ANYONE to know what I was doing.

You have to remember that vlogging wasn't a normal thing! No one was even watching vlogs back then, let alone creating them... what the heck would people think if they knew what I was doing?!?!

I did my best to make sure no one found out. I decided to create an account on YouTube under a name none of my friends would ever be able to link back to me. It took me ages to think of one — until I thought... what kind of videos am I actually going to make? Is anyone going to bother **watching them?** Doing this is literally pointless... and that was it!! **Pointless!** And what was I creating?! Video blogs...

And at that very moment

POINTLESSBLOG
was born hahaha!!

The reason I decided to create my own YouTube channel on that particular day was because I was bored bored bored!

The rain was pouring down outside and I couldn't get out of the house. So what did I make my very first video on?? 'What To Do On A Rainy Day!' Hahaa! The only thing I actually remember from this video (luckily, because it was sooo embarrassing I wouldn't want to remember any more details) was that I played Monopoly against myself... yep one of my ideas of what to do on a rainy day was to literally play Monopoly ALONE... great **video** Alfie!

SCAN
HERE

IT WAS SO STRANGE... I LITERALLY DIDN'T KNOW WHAT TO DO OR SAY!

Six of us decided to go to the cinema (can't quite remember what we went to see), but as we left something happened that will stick with me for the rest of my life (remember at this point my friends didn't know I made videos).

As we were walking out of my local Odeon cinema I heard someone behind me say 'Alfie?'... I turned around expecting to see a friend or family member... but no one I knew was there. 'It's Alfie, right? I watch your videos, man.'

... SOMEONE RECOGNISED ME FROM MY YOUTUBE VIDEOS!!

I had 1,600 people subscribed to my YouTube channel, but never did I think someone in the street – someone I didn't know – would actually care enough about my videos to stop ME and ask for a photo!!

But this wasn't the only thing rushing through my head!! My friends... my friends didn't know I made YouTube videos!? What do I say to them? How do I explain this? I don't even fully know what's going on... it doesn't feel real and now I have to try and explain the situation.

I was so overwhelmed with everything going on. I spent around 20 minutes chatting to the three boys who stopped to say hello, as well as let them help me explain to my friends what I was doing. I'm not going to lie: having people stop me in the street because they watch my videos was a pretty damn good way for my friends to find out what I'd been up to in my spare time!

COLLEGE YEARS

Leaving Varndean School to start at Varndean College was a real step forward into reality! Not only was I leaving somewhere I'd attended each and every day of my life for the past 5 years, but I was also leaving behind so many amazing teachers and friends.

I knew I'd still see them often, but it wasn't going to be the same as sitting with all my friends in one room every day. But I ~~xxxxxx~~ guess that's part of growing up! Learning to physically move away from people and still keep the friendship as strong as before is tricky, but so valuable.

Picking subjects to study is strange because you have so many different people giving you their opinion on why they think you should be picking a certain subject, but you know what really matters? What YOU want to do!

The reason you're picking these subjects to study is because you might want to continue learning/ working in that field in the future.

Choose the subjects you love not the ones you think you should be learning!

I'VE always BEEN VERY LUCKY IN THE RESPECT THAT I HAVEN'T REALLY *FOUND MAKING NEW FRIENDS TOO DIFFICULT.*

I've always surrounded myself with people similar to me and as soon as I arrived at college, I did that straight away.

One thing that was pretty weird when starting college was having a different timetable to the usual 8:45am – 3:15pm that I was used to at school. Some days I'd be working at college from 8:45am – 4:30pm and others I wouldn't even have a lesson that day! And on others I'd be in at lunchtime and finish after just two hours or so. Should I even write about revising? I found it SO difficult to concentrate by myself and revise. Like sooo difficult!

I remember one time I even spent £250 on noise-cancelling headphones JUST so I couldn't hear anyone else in the college library and get distracted and talk to them... Yeah, you guessed it... they didn't stop me! I mean, I'd spend hours each day in the college library attempting to revise, but would just end up chatting to my friends...

Just a bit of advice: **REVISE! REVISE! REVISE!** There's no point studying a subject if you're not going to work hard to get the best grade possible! The only person you're letting down is yourself...

Revision Notes

CONVINCING MY PARENTS WAS THE HARDEST THING!

I was going to write 'hours and hours', but that just wouldn't be true! So lets **start with** '**months and months**'...

...Months and months were spent persuading my parents that allowing me to buy a Vespa motorbike would somehow be a good and responsible idea! Yes I know they are dangerous, etc.

But I've always been a sensible person and... well, actually, why am I telling you why I should have one? haha!

I finally managed to persuade my parents into agreeing that it would be an 'okay' idea, not a 'good' one, but they approved enough for me to go ahead and purchase one for myself!

I'd saved up enough money from working and found the perfect one online. Being able to drive where I wanted when I wanted gave me so much freedom!

It also allowed me to set my alarm later each morning because driving to college and work on my Vespa took literally 3 minutes! I'm sure my mum ended up loving it too! It meant she no longer had to drop me at my friends' houses, etc.

I WAS THE ONLY ONE WHO THOUGHT THIS WAS A GOOD IDEA...

The only job I've ever had (I don't count my paper round, as my parents did most of it hahaa) was working part-time in a retail shop. And when I say 'part-time'... I literally mean around 4-8 hours a week, maybe 12 if I was lucky! I was paid lower than the minimum wage, but to be honest I wasn't even that bothered because I used to have so much fun working. I'd mess about with the other staff so much, try on all the clothes and make my own work outfits from the shopping bags...

So not only was I going to college every day, and working a part time job, but I was also spending hours every day creating my little videos for YouTube! Whiiiicchhh kinda meant I had no time left to revise...

I had been made part of what was called the 'YouTuber Partnership Program', which allowed YouTubers to have advertisements at the beginning of their videos and earn a tiny amount of money every time someone watched one. I was only getting a couple of thousand views per video, so it never really amounted to much... But one particular month was different. I remember the moment so vividly like *it was yesterday!*

I received my monthly email telling me how much money I'd made from YouTube on the same day as my weekend job sent me a letter in the post *telling me how much* I'd made from working there. It turns out my YouTube videos had earned me over £2 MORE than my actual real life job haha!

A normal person would see this situation as: AMAZING! NOW I GET TO EARN DOUBLE AS MUCH AS I WAS PREVIOUSLY EARNING WHEN WORKING JUST MY WEEKEND JOB!

Then, of course, there's how I read it:

AMAZING! NOW I'M **EARNING** MORE FROM YOUTUBE, I CAN QUIT MY WEEKEND JOB AND SPEND ALL MY TIME JUST MAKING VIDEOS!

Annnnnd that's what I did! Despite EVERYONE around me telling me that quitting my weekend job was a stupid decision... I went in the very next day and handed my notice in!

I'VE always BEEN CONFIDENT IN WHAT I DO.

I think one of the most important things in life is to be comfortable and confident in your own skin. It sounds so simple, but I honestly don't think I know many people who are completely comfortable within themselves.

If you want something, go and get it! If you want to change something, go and change it!

I'll always put my time into things I love doing. You can see this from me putting more time into creating YouTube videos than I did into revising for subjects I didn't enjoy at school! Or me quitting work as soon as YouTube paid me slightly more!

Most of all you've got to believe in yourself! Believe that what you're doing is right and WILL work out. Not might, not hopefully... it WILL!

the ONLY moment REALLY you HAVE is RIGHT NOW so, MAKE THE MOST OF it

SCAN HERE

YOU KNOW WHAT'S WEIRD? THINKING THAT, BEFORE YOUTUBE, I DIDN'T HAVE SOME OF THE AMAZING FRIENDS I DO TODAY.

As my audience grew on YouTube, I began to speak to other people who made YouTube videos more and more. I remember speaking to Marcus Butler when we both had less than 300 subscribers!

I was amazed that someone who lived so close to me also made YouTube videos. Chatting via DMs on Twitter we agreed to meet up and shoot a few videos together — which was weird because I'd never filmed with ANY friends before and now I was agreeing to film with someone I'd **never even met or spoken to in person...**

In fact the first time Marcus asked me where I lived I answered 'Lewes', which is a little town about 15 minutes away from where I actually lived. I didn't want him to turn out to be a creep and know where I lived haha! Annnd then when we came to actually ~~film~~ film together, I had to **explain why** I wasn't travelling from Lewes and in fact I only lived 5 minutes away from him!

It was strange. Within no time I went from hanging out with other YouTubers purely to make videos and do live shows together to going shopping, to the cinema and out for dinner.

SCAN HERE

These people were no longer 'YouTube friends' but just normal friends of mine that I happened to meet from creating videos. It was also so refreshing being able to properly speak about video ideas, views and getting recognised with people who fully understood exactly where I was coming from.

As you can probably guess by now I didn't exactly put all my time into getting the best grades at college. In fact, I was so caught up in creating YouTube videos, going to meetings about my YouTube videos and helping YouTube create new features on the site, that my college teachers told me that if I had work I needed to get done for YouTube, I could

miss my lessons!!

I was literally told by my teachers that I could make YouTube videos instead of attending lessons and they would understand!

Of course I still went to the vast majority of them and worked hard whilst at college, but if I neeeeeded to film something for a company I was working with, or had an important meeting during the day, I had the option to miss the occasional lesson.

It kinda made me feel that everyone was wanting me to succeed and do well with this little YouTube thing I spent so many hours each day doing!

I don't know why I'm writing this really, but it's just a funny little story that I'd like to write down so that I don't forget it in the future.

How to create Youtube videos

GETTING TO KNOW ZOE

Zoe and I **had been** speaking for 2 or 3 months via Skype and texting etc, but since we lived three and a half hours away from each other, it's not like we could pop out to spend time together. Oh yeah and the fact that I couldn't drive — that would have been **helpful!**

It was the 17th September (my 19th birthday), my family had all gone to work and as usual I was Skyping Zoe, telling her about **the presents my family had given me.**

Suddenly I heard a knock at the door, but I wasn't expecting anyone to be coming over... Zoe started laughing as I jumped off my bed and walked downstairs to see who it was. I opened the door to see a pizza deliveryman standing in front of me. **He passed me a massive box, smiled and walked away... Instantly I knew Zoe was up to something** haha! I ran upstairs, jumped back on the bed and showed Zoe the box and saw her little face smiling back! 'Happy Birthday Alfie!' she said. I opened the box to see my favourite pizza — tuna and sweet corn (I know its a weird mix, but it's so so delicious).

Anyyywayysss as I said I'm purely writing this down so that I don't forget this **little story in the future!**

YESTERDAY WILL always BE in the PAST & TOMORROW WILL always BE the FUTURE

RANDOM Facts:

- I've never tried a cigarette

- I've never tried ANY drugs

- I was born with a weird patch of black hair at the front of my head

- I get obsessed with things super-easy

- I've only ever been in two relationships

- I spend ALL of my time making YouTube videos

- I'm super-close with my family

Here's one thing I don't want
to forget in the future...

HERE'S SOME LIFE ADVICE:

If you ever get asked to go bungee jumping say NO!

So Marcus and I were asked if we wanted to go bungee jumping — no wait, that's not even true!
Marcus was meant to be the one doing the jumping and I was just in the video with him, but not jumping myself (so glad I wasn't asked... I would have been way too scared).

So we arrived at the highest bungee jump in the UK and I spend the first 10 minutes laughing my head off at Marcus because he was so scared! We sat down in a little tent chatting to the instructors about safety regulations when out of nowhere one of the camera crew turns to me and says 'oh yeah... I forgot to tell you that we booked you in to jump as well. Wait a second... what?! The team has booked ME in to jump without even asking or telling me! There was no chance, literally NO CHANCE I was to risk my life and jump off!

Well, that was until I saw a group of six teenage girls all giggling away to one another about how much 'fun' it was... Yep they'd just done the jump! They were sooo young, yet not scared at all! So I had to do it.

Immediately after seeing the girls, I signed all the forms with Marcus, had our harness put on us and before I knew it, I was walking up THE scariest stairs I've ever seen in my life... I'm not even joking, I thought I was going to die. **They were** so wobbly and the higher up we got, the more the wind t**hrew us around.**

I remember saying to Marcus... why are we even doing this? It's not fun at all. I feel like I'm about to jump to my death, man!

Marcus went first and swan dived perfectly over the edge! Next it was my turn. I stood up and hobbled over to the edge (my feet were strapped together and the bungee rope was attached to my ankles). As I got closer and closer, a man standing on the edge said to me 'don't look down, just ~~just~~ KEEP looking straight ahead...'

I instantly looked down.

Why I didn't listen to him, I'll never know...

You see, jumping off something is easy. Blocking out the fact that you're about to jump off one of the tallest bungee jumps in the UK and hoping your bungee cable doesn't break and that you don't just just splat on the floor below... that's the hard bit! It's ALL mental.

I threw myself over the edge annnnnd I don't really remember much else apart from spinning and spinning and spinning as I was dangling over the water below me, before waiting for the little boat to drive over and lower me down back to the ground.

As soon as I landed the two men on the boat were cheering and jumping up and down...

'NICE FLIP MAN!'

'YOU SHOULD HAVE TOLD US YOU WERE GOING TO FRONT FLIP!'

Sorry, what...? I did a front flip? Haha!

Turns out I dived off of the edge and, as I was falling, I performed a front flip! I used to perform flips and somersaults all the time when I did gymnastics, so I guess I instinctively performed a flip in the air. Not that I remember...

To be honest, it didn't even look cool! I looked like a floppy mess falling off a bridge! And that's why I'm writing this: to tell you that there's simply no fun or enjoyment in bungee jumping and don't ever bother doing it, hahaha!

FIRST BIG YOUTUBE MEET UP

I can't really describe what meeting those who watch my YouTube videos is like. I suppose the only way to describe it would be like making a friend online and then finally meeting that person in real life! Whenever people stop me to say hello in the street, they're so happy and full of energy. No matter what kind of mood you're in, it's impossible not to smile and get excited, and because of this a few friends and I thought we'd hold a meet up where viewers could meet us in person.

We promoted the event over social media, but never really knew if people would actually turn up, or care enough to travel to see us...

But as we walked towards the meeting point in the park, we could see soooo many people!! It was crazy — actually MAD! As we got closer and closer the screams were intense and every-one started running towards us! I couldn't believe what was going on. Little me who makes silly videos in my bedroom now had hundreds of people here just to see me, how crazy is that!?

We spent hours and hours hanging out, taking pictures and filming videos and although there were a LOT of people, everyone was so supportive, friendly and relaxed (after the initial few minutes haha). It felt like we were hanging out with loads and loads of friends at once. No one was more important than anyone else and the atmosphere was just so friendly and fun! It was amazing to spend time with everyone and say thank you for watching our videos.

There were more people than this

I'll never forget the feeling I felt when walking towards the park expecting to see 10, maybe 15 people, and then out of nowhere seeing the excited faces of hundreds and hundreds of people! This was for sure one of the first moments where I felt purely overwhelmed and shocked by the little online community I'd created!

NOT SUCH A GOOD DAY FOR ME...

As you know I'm not great at revising, so you can imagine AS Level results day was never going to be a great day for me, haha! I write 'haha' because I literally spent half of the day laughing – I didn't really know what else to do! When I'm nervous I often laugh... even when I'm in a situation where I really shouldn't be laughing!

My friend Holly and I walked up to receive our results together. Both of us knew we weren't going to have the best results and were already regretting wasting so much time not revising! We said to one another that whatever results we received, we wouldn't judge each other and wouldn't be sad if we didn't get the grades we wanted.

3, 2, 1 OPEN...my hands froze and I literally couldn't open the envelope! I wanted to open them somewhere with just us so that no one else was there to ask me what grades I received.

You know that annoying thing that ALWAYS happens when someone REALLY smart from your class comes up to you and says 'so what result did you get?'

And I say, 'Errmm a "B"'

And they say, 'No way, congrats! That's so, so good.'

'Oh thanks! **What** did you get?'

And they say, '...Ohh, **not great, I only** got an "A" but wanted an "A*"'

DON'T EVER BE THAT PERSON!

Anyways, Holly and I decided to go to the school library. We sat down and opened our results together... and I'm going to be honest, I really didn't do too great! Buuuut it was all my fault – I spent all my spare time watching/creating YouTube videos so what else was I ~~expecting~~ expecting?!

Holly and I walked back to my house and decided to just watch a film and give ourselves some time for our results to sink in, hoping that it'd kick our butts into revising more in the future...

I'VE ALWAYS BEEN TORN BETWEEN LIKING AND DISLIKING THE SOUND OF GOING TO UNIVERSITY.

I love learning about topics that interest me, but am not so keen on the whole exam system, and how if you wrote one extra sentence in an exam, it could change the outcome of your entire grade, and even your future career. Surely there's a better way to measure skill and intelligence?! And let's not lie: people only learn stuff to pass the exam and then forget half of the things they learnt after taking the test!

Before my exams

after my exams

My parents are both academic, with my dad studying at Oxford purely for fun and then going to another top university afterwards. My ~~dear~~ sister Poppy studied fine art at uni and scored a first in most of her exams, so I had a lot to live up to haha! I'd always joked that I was the smarter child... but here I was spending ALL my time creating videos for YouTube whilst Poppy was doing sooo well at uni!

I've always been incredibly lucky to have such supportive parents who have always let me take my own path and do what I love. I'm sure they would have wanted me to go to university and get a degree, but at the same time they could see how much fun I was having creating videos, and could see that it was my passion.

So yeah. Unless I was going to uni to make new friends and learn new life skills, I wasn't really into the idea. However, just in case I changed my mind, I applied to a top media university in London. It was something completely different to anything I'd ever studied before (Maths and Science), but I thought, as I enjoyed making YouTube videos so much, I'd rather spend three years at uni learning more about that kind of thing.

WHAT I'M ABOUT TO SAY COULDN'T SUM UP MY LIFE ANY MORE IF I TRIED!!

After traveling for two hours, I arrived at Ravensbourne University in London for my interview. It was weirdly empty; I first thought maybe everyone was sat in a separate waiting room before their own interview? Or that maybe I was the last person of the day?

I walked over to the check-in desk and presented the woman with my interview form. She looked confused and said 'Erm, the interviews were ~~actually~~ actually yesterday' and pointed to the date at the top of my OWN printed out piece of paper! Yep I'd literally turned up the day after all the interviews! Typical Alfie!

She asked me to go take a seat whilst she called up stairs to see if the man who was holding all of the interviews happened to be in to have a chat with me... I felt like such an idiot! What a great first impression! Turning up on the wrong day!

Somehow the man holding the interviews happened to be in and was even free to have an interview with me in his office! Phew! I jumped in the lift and went up to his office to meet him. You know what's even funnier? When applying for a creative subject at university, you're asked to bring your portfolio of work, including work from previous media classes you'd taken at college or school. I'd kinda never done any media lessons before, so I took my laptop and some of my YouTube videos with me haha!

We chatted about YouTube, the future of TV/the Internet and why I like making videos, for about 20 minutes. I remember, just as the interview was coming to an end, he said 'One last question Alfie. What do you feel is going to be the next big thing in the technology world?' or something along those lines. And I answered: I think 3D TVs will become normal and people will be able to have them in their own houses, not just at the cinema. (Fast forward to now and I have two 3D TVs in my house! I was right!).

I honestly couldn't believe what happened next! Right there and then, I was offered a position at the university! He literally said 'Although I'm not actually allowed to tell you this as it's only *the interview*, I'd like to offer you a place at Ravensbourne University because the aim of the course is to get you out there into the world of media and you're already out there doing that.'

TYPICAL ALFIE:

TURN UP ON THE WRONG DAY FOR MY INTERVIEW.

SOMEHOW **MANAGE** TO GET AN INTERVIEW.

GET OFFERED A PLACE AT THE UNIVERSITY THERE AND THEN!

I don't know how I get away with this stuff!

My final A-level exams were just a few weeks away and I still hadn't started revising. YouTube was taking up all of my spare time and I didn't want to give it up because I was having sooo much fun doing it and it was actually starting to go somewhere! Whilst all my friends had their heads tucked into books, I had my head in front of my laptop screen...

I ended up revising for *1 hour per exam*... I had 10 exams and only did 10 hours of revision.

NEVER DO THIS!!

I honestly sat in some of my exams asking myself why I didn't revise more, but there was nothing I could do! It was too late to realise that!

You know what I hate? When you come out of a Maths or Science exam and ask your friends what they wrote for one of the questions, hoping they'd reply with what you answered! Then they say something different to me but similar to each other. That's when I knew I'd messed up.

RESULTS DAY.

For sure one of the scariest moments of my life! I felt so sick!

To receive my A level results, all I had to do was log into the college ~~system~~ system from home any time after 7am and my results would be waiting there for me, along with the result of my university application.

I sat down with my family, nervously logged into the college system and clicked through to see if I'd been accepted into University or not...All that was running through my head was 'Alfie why didn't you revise more?! Buuuuut it was too late to worry about that — there was nothing that could change my results now!

'CONGRATULATIONS'

Wait, sorry, what?!?... I'd somehow been accepted into university!! But I hadn't revised? I found my exams sooo hard? What? When? How? Hahaa!!

I was sooo confused – surely I hadn't fluked all my exams and somehow got the grades I needed to get into uni? That's literally impossible!

I scrolled further down to reveal my A-level results for each subject (Maths, Chemistry and Geography). Something was wrong – something was weird! I scrolled back up and refreshed the page.

'CONGRATULATIONS'

But I hadn't scored high enough results to get into my university course... Yet it still said I had been accepted? Grabbing my mobile, I gave the university a call, because I didn't want to celebrate if there was some kind of mistake! **And that's when yet another one of those weird moments happened to me, when I get** incredibly lucky... It was right, I HAD been accepted! But what the heck, I didn't get good enough A-level results?

After speaking to the woman on the phone for a good 10 minutes, she told me I'd impressed the leader of the course (the man who interviewed me) so much that he gave me an unconditional offer!! Whatttttt!? That basically meant that whatever A level results I got, I was guaranteed a place on the course because the university wanted ME on the course!!

I WAS **ACCEPTED INTO UNIV**ERSITY WITHOUT HAVING TO REVISE!!

... this definitely isn't a photo of me wearing my sister's graduation gown.

MALFIE BREAKING RECORDS

Ever since I can remember I've been obsessed with the Guinness World Records books, receiving the newest one every year from my mum and dad. If you were to visit my parents' house, you'd see the books all lined up in order, starting in 1996 (I think).

The reason I like *the book* so much is because it's about being the best in the world! If you get your name in the book, it means no one else is better than you at that given thing! Wait... since we don't have proof that aliens exist, technically if you have a Guinness world record, you're the best in the universe! How cool is that!?!
Out of all 7 billion people, no one can do that thing better than YOU!

Since reading my first copy of the book I've always told my parents that I'll be in there one day! Of course it'd be for something stupid and weird, but I'd be in there one day! Growing up I'd practice all my weird little talents like solving a Rubik's cube or dice stacking, just in case it was my calling and I'd somehow make the book!

Well, fast forward to 2012, Marcus and I received an email asking if we'd be interested in presenting a new YouTube channel for Guinness World Records!! Each week we'd be attempting to break a different funny world record on camera.

This was my chance to be in the book!!

Marcus and I had never filmed with a proper camera crew or even in a studio! For these videos we had our own paramedics in case something went wrong, along with our own make up artists, lighting team, audio man, camera team with three different cameras running at all times, and a Guinness official watching over us! Basically it was a LOT different to anything

Guinness World Records
SLATE:
100
MARCUS BUTLER
ALFIE DEYES

129

we'd ever done before, but it was exciting and something for us to learn and try out! But best of all we'd be learning it all together and having fun at the same time.

We filmed for a good two weeks but still didn't break any records! If it was just Marcus and I it would have been funny, but obviously it was all being filmed!! I can't even describe how much Marcus, the team and myself wanted to actually break a record!

Occasionally we'd have guests on for an episode to give them a chance to break a record (which was also unsuccessful haha). FunForLouis was on set and we were attempting to break a record for most party poppers popped in 30 seconds. Marcus went first, but unfortunately didn't make it; next was Louis, who also didn't make the cut and lastly, it was my turn to try and break the record. Considering we'd spent the whole day filming — in fact the whole week — filming record attempts, the pressure was on! And then, out of nowhere, I only went and beat it, popping 29 poppers in half a minute!! Hahaa yes it wasn't the most impressive record, BUT it was a record!! An official Guinness world record! I was going to be in the next book and in my mind that was enough to make childhood Alfie proud!

Over the next few weeks Marcus and I broke soooo many funny records! A few times I'd attempt a record first, break it and then Marcus would go next and beat my just-made record, instantly taking it away from me!

I think, overall, I had/have (not sure how many of ours have been beaten since we attempted them) nine records and Marcus has/had ten!

I was so excited to attempt to break all of those records on YouTube. But looking back on it, the most valuable thing I gained wasn't the records themselves, but the opportunity to hang out with Marcus for 6 weeks and spend more time with a friend. And then also gaining the experience of working with a big camera team and getting used to filming high production videos!

What records do you want to break?

I WAS SOOO BUSY DURING THE SUMMER AFTER COLLEGE, MAKING YOUTUBE VIDEOS AND FLYING AROUND THE PLACE TO VARIOUS DIFFERENT MEET UPS!

I was still 'living' at home with my parents, although I was basically living out of a suitcase due to traveling so much and doing **YouTube videos.** I tried my best to spend every moment back home with either friends or family, to make sure **that my relationships back in Brighton** weren't affected due to YouTube. I'd literally film all day in London, get back to Brighton late in the evening, go out for dinner/ clubbing with friends and then head back to do more filming early the next morning.

Friends and family have always been super-important to me. I'm the friend who will call you at 10pm and say 'let's go do something fun!!' and you'll probably be in bed asleep haha! The amount of times I persuaded friends to get out of bed and come out for a late dinner/to go clubbing that summer was mad. It was the only way I could really spend proper time with **friends back home,** since I was mostly out of Brighton working on YouTube videos.

A midnight McDonald's with my friend Holly was always a good shout! We'd rock up in pyjamas and eat soo much food it'd put us to sleep haha!

SUMMER WAS AMAZING!

The freedom of being able to make YouTube videos as my full time 'job' was unreal. I inserted the marks around 'job' because I still don't really count it as my real job. It's more like a hobby of mine that I'm fortunate enough to earn enough money from. It's basically the same as it being just a hobby, except I don't have to go to work during the day and instead I can spend all my time working on new videos and projects!

Anyywayyyss summer was so good! It really opened up my eyes and showed me that maybe these videos could be my actual full-time job for a while. So I took a big step and decided to defer university for a year! Which basically means 'Thank you for offering me a place, but I'm going to have a year out of education and I'll come to university next year'.

Most people would take this time to grab a big rucksack, stuff it with important things and travel the world hoping to learn life lessons and to 'find themselves'... and then there's me! I took a year out to spend more time working on making videos and hanging out with friends haha! Don't get me wrong, I was technically 'working' ~~maybe~~ because YouTube was my job, but I didn't see it like that! I saw it as a year with no lessons, to have fun and hang out with friends!

I'D rather SPEND MY TIME BUILDING my OWN Dreams than SPENDING MY Time Building Someone ELSE'S

THIS WAS PROBABLY ONE OF THE BIGGEST DECISIONS OF MY LIFE SO FAR!

My mum is one of those mums who loves to do everything for you. She actually enjoys looking after me and helping me with things like washing my clothes or dropping me off at friends' houses. So the idea of leaving home to live by myself was kinda **scary!** I literally had no idea how to cook, clean and pay bills! Basically everything you need to be **able to** do when living by yourself haha!

So instead of going solo I decided it would be a better idea to live with someone who's in the exact same position as me and also knows **absolutely nothing** about living by themselves...

So I decided to move in with Caspar Lee! Caspar was living in South Africa at the time, but we had met a few

times before through making **YouTube** videos together with friends.

So he flew over to London, jumped on a train to Brighton **annndd** we **kinda just decided on everything then and there once he was here haha!** It sounds like I'm exaggerating and it was more planned than this, but it honestly wasn't!

He arrived in Brighton and planned to live with my parents for as long as it took us to find a flat to move in together! A few days after Caspar arrived, we jumped on a train up to London **and booked in a few flat viewings.** The second place we went to see was perfect! We made an offer and agreed to move in **the NEXT day!!**

Everything was going so perfectly!! Soon we'd be living together, **making videos all day every day annnd** be in London! (Which if you don't know, is only 55 minutes away from Brighton so I could easily visit friends and family **anytime I wanted**).

Now...we had to somehow survive without our parents — **which was something neither of us knew** how to do — and we more or less ended up living on stir-fries, **takeaways and pasta for the first few months,** because that's all we knew how to cook (or at least I know how!)

I'M SAT HERE LAUGHING WHILST WRITING THIS!

I remember one time I was at the Sugg family house when Zoe received a FaceTime call from Caspar. (Sorry to Caspar in advance for embarrassing you haha! But it really sums up our time living together!)

Caspar called Zoe to ask her how to make pasta. Not even a pasta sauce; literally plain pasta! Like pasta from a packet!! He didn't know whether to use boiled water, cold water and heat it, or just cold water!

We were useless! We didn't even know how to wash our clothes. Of course we had a washing machine, we just didn't know how to use it. Wait actually I tried once! I washed 4 pairs of jeans and they all came out tiny and shriveled... so every time I used to visit my parents back in Brighton, I'd take a massive suitcase full of dirty clothes and my mum'd wash and iron them for me... this was at the age of 20! My mum's the best mum in the world! haha! But it really sums up our time living together!

There were loads of things Caspar and I got up to — too many to write down here... wait, one last one **haha!**
I remember one time we thought it'd be a good idea for us to both join a gym and start working out together each morning. We searched online and found a local gym a five-minute jog away.
A few **days later we bought new** gym clothes, jogged down to the gym and both bought *three-month* memberships. **Yeahhh that was kinda the only time I went and** I think Caspar went once without me... what a waste! haha!

SCAN HERE

I DIDN'T HAVE a CLUE WHAT TO EXPECT!

After creating YouTube videos for a few years and occasionally attending the odd meet and greet, a group of us (Zoe, Marcus, Tanya, Jim, Louise and Caspar) decided it was about time to properly get out there and meet those who watch what we do. We'd already met a bunch of viewers who lived in the UK at various events and YouTube meets and greets, so I thought it'd be a good idea to travel ~~and~~ abroad this time! We never really knew what to expect – yes people watch our videos, but paying money and traveling to meet us in person is completely different! Would anyone actually bother coming to see us?

We all **had a very large audience in America** so we **thought** it was only right to fly over there for the tour and whilst we were so close to Canada, we added it into the tour too!

Each venue was between 2,000 **and 3,000 seats**, which thinking about it now, was crazy! They sold tickets out in minutes. Literally minutes! It was so, so mad!

00:00:43

We all sat down and started to plan what we were going to do on stage to make the show engaging and fun, but at the same time similar to our videos. It took days and days to plan our hour-long stage show; we had to make sure it would be good enough to perform in front of so many people at once! I can't quite remember who came up with the idea, but along the way we decided it'd be a good idea to bring special guests along to each of our shows to surprise the audience and bring a different element e.g singers/dancers etc!

It was all planned and ready to go and all that was left was to wait for the date to actually come about, and for us seven friends to fly across the world and officially be on tour!! A YouTube Tour!!

TIME TO FLY across THE WORLD WITH MY
FRIENDS aND BEGIN OUR TOUR!

TOUR - Car MOBBED - FLiGHtS
EVERY MORNING - FaNS EVERYWHERE

SCAN
HERE

I LOVE TRYiNG NEW THiNGS,

but when you've got a few million eyes watching your every move, it's kinda hard to 'try' something because if you fail, well, it's not the best haha!

So me being me, and putting more work on myself, I decided to start a gaming channel on YouTube! Not the typical games like Halo, which I played loads while growing up, but more funny and stupid games. Such as showing my embarrassing dancing skills on Just Dance or failing at Minecraft, where I'd record myself playing the game on my camera and at the same time record the screen of my game so everyone watching the video could see what was going on. Then I'd edit the two together so you can see the game and my reaction to me playing it.

Gaming was and still is SO popular on YouTube, so I knew there was an audience that might be interested in these gaming videos of mine, but wasn't sure if the audience that watched my vlogs would be interested in them.

...And then I started playing Sims with **Zoe!**

Growing up I'd always played hours and hours and hours of Sims with Poppy. We had every single expansion pack in a row next to our family computer! And back then, I swear there were like **15 expansions or something!**

Anyways, I thought Sims would be a good game to play on my new gaming channel, since it's kind of like daily vlogging, but talking instead about your fake family haha! The people watching my videos could help me decide what to build in the game and which jobs to give the characters — it was a joint effort. Zoe, who loved the game growing up, would sit and play with me too. Annnd let's just say it went **down well** haha! Each little video of Zoe sitting on my lap (as I only had one office chair) playing Sims would hit millions and millions of views!!

SOME OF THE BEST THINGS IN LIFE COME AT THE MOST RANDOM OF TIMES!

For example once, when a few of us YouTubers were having dinner, Marcus, Joe and I were sitting at one end of the table singing this song non-stop... agh I can't remember which one! But it was an old classic. Literally the entire meal we were crying, laughing and singing it together. After we'd all finished up eating and were sitting around the table chatting, we somehow came up with the idea of how funny it would be if we made a parody style boy band called 'The YouTube Boyband'.

Marcus, Jim, Joe and I headed up to Marcus' hotel room, balanced his camera and tripod on a little side table so it was **tall enough for us to stand** up and dance in front of... and that's where it all began.

There was no plan; we hit the record button and freestyled everything. Well I say that, but from the shockingly bad/funny video, it's pretty damn obvious that none of us knew what we were doing. We were ~~singing~~ singing and dancing for literally an hour, non-stop. Oh and I should point out it was like 3am, I have no idea how we didn't get kicked out of the hotel that night!

And for some reason, when Marcus put the video up online that weekend, people went **CRAZY!**

My comments and tweets online for the next few months were FULL of people asking for more boy band videos or photos.

What the heck had we started? haha!

I HAD SO MUCH FUN LIVING IN LONDON WITH CASPAR FOR EIGHT MONTHS OR SO, BUT IT ALSO SHOWED ME THAT LONDON LIFE WASN'T REALLY FOR ME.

I was used to living in a city where everyone knew each other and in a place where I could see family and friends in a matter of minutes if I wanted.

Whereas London was so busy, I'd literally wake up tired! I wouldn't have even done anything except walk to a cafe to grab breakfast and I'd feel tired from the amount of people everywhere.

Caspar also wanted to have a break from London and go back to South Africa for a few months, get some sun and see his family.

So we decided to hand in our notice to our landlord and enjoy the last few months of living together before he flew back to South Africa and I moved back to Brighton.

Back on the south coast, I moved into a flat on my own, which was weird because although Caspar wasn't any good at household chores, being alone meant I didn't even have someone who I could ask to see if I was washing my clothes right or whether I was using the right dishwasher tablets haha.

The main thing I enjoyed about living alone was the silence. That makes me sound so boring and weird, but there's something I find relaxing about my own company. I could do what I wanted when I wanted — such as walk around with no clothes on or dance to really loud music because it wouldn't wake up or affect anyone else. It was just me!

YOU KNOW THAT WEIRD BOYBAND THING WE DID AS A JOKE IN THAT HOTEL ROOM FOR MARCUS' YOUTUBE CHANNEL? WELL THINGS WERE ABOUT TO STEP UP A LEVEL.

A few months after filming our stupid hotel room singing video, we received a call from Richard Curtis and Emma Freud asking us to pop over to their **house for dinner and discuss an exciting** project. Of course we all said we'd love to, in fact Zoe and Tanya also came along, we all hung out, played with their family cat a lot (it's the cutest thing ever) and eventually, after stuffing our faces with **food and cake, got talking about this project!**

*As you can **tell from** what you've read of this book so far, I'm not the best at writing, so I'm not going to try and explain the entire evening to you... so I'll summarise the outcome*

We (The YouTube BoyBand) were asked to record a song with a music video and **everything to raise money for Sport Relief!! The song** and video would be professionally recorded in London and would go live on YouTube for everyone to see!

One slight issue... could any of us actually sing?

Appreciate every MINUTE of EVERY DAY AS YOU never KNOW what TOMORROW BRINGS

RECORDING OUR VERY FIRST SONG...

Turning up, we had literally no idea what to expect. As we walked into the recording studio, we were told that a number of different artists had recorded massive songs in the exact same place.

I couldn't help but hope that someone had warned the recording team that we weren't actually singers and we were simply doing it for charity.

All the boys squished up together on one little sofa next to the sound engineer's table... or I'm guessing it was something like that haha. It had so many buttons on it I swear it would be nearly impossible for one person to even know what they all do!

We started running through the song with each of us singing our parts out loud, just to warm up and let the sound team know who was singing which parts etc.

And then it was time... I, for sure, did not want to embarrass myself by going first! ...Wait, have I actually mentioned how bad I am at singing? Yeah let's just say pretty damn awful! Watching the boys sing their lines in the little 'audio booth room' (I'm just making up all these terms as they sound right haha) it was my turn.

I did my part and tried to just have as much fun as possible by remembering the reason I was there, not to sound good, but to raise awareness and money for Sport Relief.

The hardest bit for me was not knowing what any of the other boys sounded like. The sound man kept playing parts back and saying things like 'go just a little lower/higher on that note' etc.

But not knowing how low/high/good I was scared me and I'd have to wait a few days until we shot the music video to listen to the final mix of the song.

157

The song had been recorded/mixed together and was ready for the YouTube boyband to hear for the very first time!

As we walked into this massive studio, it kinda hit me how awesome this music video and song was actually going to be! The very first thing I saw as I entered was a MASSIVE and I mean **massive** – like taller than my house – camera crane! The crew was setting up the cameras and sorting out the different video sets. We all went straight to hair and make-up (yeah boys get make-up too when doing video shoots haha!) and the woman doing my make up got a little electronic razor out, turned it on and said 'do you mind leaning forward for me?'

Wait, sorry, what? I was so confused and asked her what she was about to do.

'Bring your hair line at the back up a bit' was her reply. If you don't know already, I'm sooo fussy about my hair and there was no way I could let someone who I'd never met before cut my hair!! So I stuck with my hair being styled instead of cut haha!

I'm glad the team producing the video knew we were there to mess about and create a fun music video for a jokey song we'd recorded, because literally, as soon as we walked in, we all started being stupid. Thinking about it, it was kinda their fault for buying sooo many funny props to use. We were riding little tricycles and tandem bikes around the place, and wearing swimming clothes whilst getting our make-up done...

In fact, Caspar spent most of the day wearing a massive faux fur coat with a giant silver chain! Let's just say we didn't exactly take the day too seriously!

We were there to have fun and create an amazing video!

Filming was going super-well: we kicked it off with all of us on stalls, sitting in a line like a proper old-school boyband music video, pretending to play different instruments. I think one of us, maybe Caspar, didn't have an instrument, so was just playing the air guitar haha!

Then we changed into some white suits... we all looked ridiculous and were laughing at how stupid each of us looked! I looked like a really bad Elvis impersonator with a few buttons undone and my collar up. We filmed all the typical camera-above-the-boyband shots, with each person taking their turn singing their lines towards the camera.

We wanted to make the video as funny and stupid as possible, since it was for charity. So we were all doing stupid things on camera and just messing about having as much fun as we could.

There was actually a lot of footage that people never properly saw. We shot this underwater scene for sooo long, pretending to swim in tiny little shorts with inflatables and flippers haha! But when the video was all edited together, I don't think any of it, or maybe only a tiny part actually made the cut. I know some of the footage is out there in the outtakes or behind the scenes, but it's funny looking back on bits like that. When shooting big videos you sometimes spend sooo long on a scene and then it never actually ends up anywhere! But I guess that's just part of it.

Anyways, we wrapped up the shoot and were all so, so excited to see the outcome. It was weird having to wait to see the music video, because with **our videos we can turn an average** edit around in an afternoon. But for this I think we waited a few weeks!

I remember *being sent the* download link to **watch the video** for the very first time. I was SO nervous. What if I didn't like it? *What if people thought* we were **actually trying to do** a proper cover and sound/look good haha?

After watching literally 10 seconds of the video, I was obsessed! It was sooo us. **So stupid, jokey and fun! Annnd,** most of all, it raised awareness and money for an amazing cause.

I REMEMBER RECEIVING a RANDOM PHONE call FROM MY MANAGER ASKING ME iF I'D BE INTERESTED IN MEETING WITH a BOOK PUBLISHER WiTH a VIEW TO WRITING a BOOK

As anyone who knows me will know, I dropped English in school as soon as I could, so writing a book wasn't exactly something I'd ever thought about or wanted to do before. So I politely declined the offer for a meeting with the publisher.

A few weeks later I got another call from the publisher, who asked to meet with me to chat through different book styles and ideas. Again I wasn't interested in writing a novel or anything because writing isn't really for me. I like creating videos!

They called back and said it doesn't have to be a novel — it could be anything I wanted it to be. I couldn't really say no to that haha! So I agreed to meet them, but made sure they knew it wasn't likely anything was going to come from us meeting up.

Myself, my manager and two members of the publishing team sat down in a tiny, tiny little meeting room and chatted through different possible ideas — none of which were remotely close to a novel!

That's when we came up with the idea of creating something similar to my YouTube videos – including lots of silly challenges and things for the readers to do themselves, just like when people recreate videos I'd made at home.

I also wanted it to be something similar to the daily vlog style videos that I created. These were like time capsules for me to look back on in the future and to see what I was thinking each day and what I liked/didn't like at the time. And since the idea for this book was for people to fill it out, they would be able to look back at it in years to come and the book itself would almost be like a time capsule of their life.

I was so excited! No other YouTubers had really done a book before and the fact that it was an extension to the videos I made, I knew (hoped haha) that the people who watched my videos, would also enjoy the book! But obviously I was nervous! I'd never asked my viewers to pay for something before. Everything I'd done was for free, so I'm not going to lie, I was pretty damn nervous to see how people were going to react.

THiS BOOK CONSUMED PRETTY MUCH THE NEXT FEW MONTHS OF MY LiFE!

Even when I was away traveling with friends, I'd be bugging them all to help me come up with ideas for each page haha!

A load of us UK YouTubers flew out to Italy for a meet up/YouTube event in Milan. It was super-exciting because although we had held meet-and-greets in the UK and America, we had never really held one anywhere else in Europe. No matter how many times I meet viewers, the amount of people who turn up and support they give is always, always, always overwhelming!

We were in Milan for three days, but that wasn't the end for the boys, we'd planned an epic road trip before going back to the UK. The girls all flew home, while the boys (me, Marcus, Joe, Caspar, Trove, Connor, Tyler and Louis) grabbed two cars for the week and set off to hit as many amazing landmarks as possible in five days before flying back from Naples (over 500 miles).

I can't even describe how nice it was to relax with so many friends at once. The long drives **from city to city were probably** my favourite **part of** the trip. I love a **deep chat with friends and trust me** we had a **good few of those!** We only had one **place booked for the** night and booked the rest of our accommodation as we drove around each day. We got to see so many incredible things — an insane winery, the Leaning Tower of Pisa, the Roman Colosseum and so much more.

Whilst we got up to all these fun things, I was planning/writing my book, and as I was surrounded by so many creative people the entire *trip*, *some of the pages you've seen in* **THE POINTLESS BOOK** *for sure came from some of the boys. So thanks for some of the ideas, guys!* I remember sitting in this little **hotel, which was a bit like a villa.** Anyway we were sat in the lobby and it was raining sooo much outside that instead of going out and exploring, we decided to all sit in the lobby for few hours and have laptop club. That lobby was the place I emailed over the very first **draft copy of book 1!**

WHILST DRIVING AROUND ITALY, WE DIDN'T REALLY HAVE A PLAN.

We had a few things we knew we wanted to see such as Pisa and Rome, and we wanted to find somewhere to get a massage. All of us (except Joe) love to get a good massage and whenever we're traveling try and get one.

We'd heard about a crazy new winery that had just been built.

Thinking about it, I don't think any of us were even big wine drinkers, but we'd seen and heard about how amazing this place was and we had no time restrictions, so drove on over.

The people working there must have thought we were right weirdos! I can imagine their usual customers are 30+ year olds who take wine very seriously and here we were... a group of 20-something year olds all filming each other and joking around.

I'm not going to lie, it was actually super-interesting! We had a member of staff show us around and explain how the wine is made etc. After the tour we headed over to the on-site **restaurant where lunch had been set up for us for free!** (Major perk of making YouTube videos!)

SCAN HERE

We tried tons of different wines whilst eating and all bought a couple of bottles on the way out.

It was such a random, but fun day with the boys! And I'll never **forget it — since then I've loved red wine!**

IT WAS TIME FOR a CHANGE.

Something new. Something challenging but rewarding. It was time to start daily vlogging!

I'd had my second YouTube channel 'PointlessBlogVlogs' for quite some time and uploaded the occasional daily log style video. I loved filming the videos but not every day of my life was fun enough to film haha!

The thing I love about daily vlogging is how the audience can properly engage with someone everyday and trust me, once you start watching someone's life, it's so addictive! So with that in mind, I thought it was about time I challenged myself to film every single day for one whole month! It doesn't sound like much, but it's not just the filming and editing, it's keeping each video entertaining enough so that people want to watch you every day!

Anyways, it was coming towards the end of one of the most fun and productive months of my life and I sat back and thought to myself... why am I stopping? The videos were storing so many great memories, plus they're great fun to put together and my viewers are loving them — why should I stop!?

So I didn't. That would have been stupid!

As I sit here writing this very sentence, I'm still, to this day, vlogging on a daily basis!

'I'M THE SMARTER SIBLING!' I always JOKED WITH POPPY GROWING UP, BUT FOR SURE THIS WASN'T TRUE!

Whilst I was **having** fun creating YouTube videos **and traveling** the world to meet people who watched me, Poppy was living in London working her butt off studying fine art at university.

I always felt bad because I was constantly having fun with friends and whenever I spoke to Poppy she was working, working, **working**.

I had to keep on reminding myself that although she had to study really hard at university, **she also** was what that she loved!

It **came down** to results day and, **of course, she went and** smashed a 1st!

Since then I kinda don't mention the 'I'm the smarter sibling' thing anymore haha! I only just passed college and she's getting the best grades possible at uni!

THiS STORY iS all aBOUT PROBaBly THE CRaZiESt DaY OF MY LiFE SO FaR...

Waking up like any other day, I ate breakfast with Zoe whilst watching YouTube videos. Zoe had a taxi booked to take her off to a work day in London and I had a book signing that lunchtime, also in London! Originally I was thinking of jumping on a train and then either a taxi or tube, but since Zoe was already heading into London, I decided it would be stupid not to jump in her taxi with her...

This was my very first book signing and I had absolutely no idea how things were going to go... or if people were even going to turn up to get their book signed! I mean, I'd mentioned it in two or ~~two~~ three daily vlogs, but since it wasn't a ticketed event, I couldn't actually tell how many people were planning on attending.

About 30 minutes into the journey and still about three or four hours away from my book signing was planned to start, my phone started ringing. It wasn't good news...I was asked to delete all my tweets about the book signing and instead tweet a message asking people to NOT come along to the signing. At this point I should point out how difficult it was for my book publishers to even get me a signing in central London!

No book stores believed that I'd be able to get people to turn up to meet me and get their books signed since I wasn't a 'traditionally known celebrity' ... In fact I'm not any kind of celeb; I just make little videos that quite a few people watch for some reason! Anyways, as my taxi turned the corner... things went pretty wrong! It wasn't just the 1,000s of people surrounding the cars outside the book store — screaming, crying and banging on the windows so hard that we thought the windows were going to break... but also the two HELICOPTERS circling above, making sure the crowds weren't getting out of control. Ohhh and the 15 policemen on horseback and countless police on foot... Yeeeahhh let's just say a few people came to get a book signed by me!

Zoe and I had literally no idea what to do. We both sat there looking at each other helpless. We were so, so, so overwhelmed. I'd never felt something quite like this before. Zoe burst into tears and I was sooo close to crying.

Not because we were scared, but purely because seeing so many people who were there to show their support for me and my new book! It was madness, like actually so amazing.

After the police helped me out of the taxi and escorted me into the building through literally a crowd of 8,500 people, I met up with my book publishers and management and we didn't even know what to say or what to think/feel. All I could think about was why did ALL these people come out of their way — get trains, drive and even fly from other countries — juuuust to meet me. I mean, yeah, I'd gone to YouTube ~~events~~ events before with loads of other vloggers, but people weren't attending them just to see me! This was different. Those who were outside the shop were here purely to meet me and get their books signed!

I only managed to meet around 500 people before a commanding officer of London's Metropolitan Police came running in and requested to speak to me. At this point there were hundreds of fans standing in queues in front of me... I had no idea what he was going to say and with sooo many people watching and recording me, I couldn't stop thinking the worst haha!

I mean **obviously I knew** I'd done nothing wrong because I never ever expected over **8,500 people to turn up,** buuuuut at the same time, **they were all outside and it was** crazy out there! He was super-calm, but said if he didn't get me out of **the building in the next 20 minutes the shop windows and doors** were going to be smashed in by my fans trying to meet me!

Sorry what?! People were legit trying to **BREAK through the doors** and **windows to get to ME!**

I carried on signing for as long as I possibly could (until the police told me I HAD to get out) after which I was driven off to a hotel on the other **side of London where my friends and family were waiting with**

drinks and food to celebrate the launch of my book!

Not going to lie, I'll never forget that day! When talking about it, it feels like I'm exaggerating or lying, but honestly! It was mad...

SCAN HERE

BEING THROWN IN THE DEEP END.

That's exactly how I felt when my first book went to #1 on the bestsellers chart. Every TV show, radio station, newspaper and **magazi**ne wanted to interview me. How was **this kid who made little YouTube videos in his bedroom** suddenly breaking the book charts haha! To be honest I **had** no clue **myself!** All I knew was that those who watched my videos were awesome and killing it!

The first interview I did was one of the early morning breakfast shows. I had to stay up north and wake up at something ridiculous like 5 or 6am to get over to the studio, meet the team, go through hair and make-up, and finally do my 6-minute live interview. I remember sitting backstage beforehand, **watching** the show on a little TV screen in front of me. I leant over to one of the snazzy headset-wearing producers next to me and asked how **many people were watching at the moment** and to be **honest, I probably** shouldn't have! I thought it'd be a few hundred thousand, maybe **a million...nope!**

Apparently over 9.5 million! Over 9 million people were about to watch me LIVE. I was used to being on camera, but I can choose what goes into my videos and if I mess up, I can edit that bit out.

Walking onto the set as they were on a commercial break, I met the two presenters who were so friendly and relaxed, it instantly calmed me down. The show started back up, we all got chatting and before I knew it, my six minutes were up and I was off on the train home! From that point, live TV didn't scare me at all, looking back on it, it couldn't have been better. Nowadays I can relax a little because I'll never be as nervous as when I first appeared in front of so many people!

The press didn't stop there. That week I went from TV shows, to radio shows, to photoshoots... to literally everything! You name a magazine/tv show/radio show and I was on it! It was unbelievable. Everyone I new back at home in Brighton was texting me saying they'd just seen me on this or that and again, it's something I'll never forget.

GROWING OLDER IS AND ALWAYS WILL BE WEIRD FOR ME.

I remember when my cousin James turned 21 and I thought, jeez, my cousin is an adult now! He's so old... like a grown up! I also remember my sister turning 21 and kinda thinking the same and yet I don't know why, I just never imagined myself becoming an adult.

I think, deep down inside, I'm still 18... actually no, only sometimes. I can be mature when I need to be — like in meetings and for business stuff — but then I love to mess about, jump up and down on *hotel beds,* when *they're* freshly made and prank call people. But maybe that's not being 'young', that's just the kind of person you are, and I'm immature sometimes. Which I think is a good fun thing to be!

I dunno what I really planned to write on this page, I just find it so weird that I'm growing older, yet I don't feel any older if that makes sense? Do you *feel the* same?

My 21st birthday was amazing. My family rented a room in one of my favourite restaurants and filled the place with awesome decorations, such as personlised placemats (made by my mum!) which included pictures of me at various stages of my young life. It felt like yesterday that I was celebrating turning 16... and yet now all of a sudden I'm 22!

What. How. When?

MOVING IN WITH ZOE

Moving house is a big deal. Whether that's your family moving, moving to university, moving in with a friend or in this case, for me, moving from living by myself to living with **my girlfriend!**

Zoe **moved down to Brighton about** a year ago into a flat on the beach and I had my own flat about 15 minutes walk away.

At first this was perfect, we could both work from our own flats and then spend the evening together, but still have our own space. Space for me is really important, don't get me wrong, I love hanging out with friends and family, but I do also love spending time to myself listening to music and working without anyone disturbing me.

However, as much as we loved spending tons of time together, the fact that we had separate flats complicated things hugely!

So as **you've guessed, we** decided to move in together!

When the day finally came for us to move in together we were both so, so excited! Everything went to plan and before we knew it, it was like we'd **never** lived separately.

MY NEW YORK BOOK SIGNING!

My American book publishers offered to fly me out to New York to do a load of press along with a massive book signing in New York and, of course, I didn't turn it down. So before I knew it, Maddie (one of my managers) and I jumped on a plane and we were on our way to the big ol' city of New York!

*wait... I'm forgetting something... or **someone***

I thought, since my mum had never been to New York before, it'd be really nice to have her come along and see what it's like to have days full of TV, radio and magazine/newspaper interviews, as well as attend her first event where people who watch my videos come to see me in person. So I booked her a ticket to come and join in!

And before we knew it, we were on a plane and on our way to **the Big Apple! I've been very** fortunate with all the traveling I've been able to do for YouTube but one thing I'd never done before was fly first class!

This was both my mum's first time and my own first time, and to say we ~~were~~ were excited would be an understatement. Only five years before I was making my first little YouTube video in my bedroom with my family camera stacked on a pile of books, and now here I was flying first class with my mum to New York to meet thousands of people who were coming to show their support for my very first book... what the heck?!!

We made the absolute most out of that flight! I spent the entire time lying flat down (because I could) and eating everything I was offered whilst watching films non-stop haha!

As soon as we landed we were picked up by one of those big blacked-out American cars (I have no idea what they're called... but the fancy-looking ones) and whisked off to do TV interviews! American press is so much fun! They're so ~~supportive~~ supportive and interested in young people who manage to turn a hobby into a job... whereas the UK press just like to ask questions about how much money you earn and whether making YouTube videos even counts as a job... stupid I know.

We only had a few days in New York, so crammed as much in for my mum to see and do as possible! She loved it!!

I never really knew what to expect with the signing – whether people in New York would be interested enough to actually come and queue up to get their book signed. I mean I knew a LOT of people came along to the signing in London, but I had no idea about New York! Yeahhhh, I was wrong as usual. There were thousands of people! But this time everything went super-smoothly and it was so, so, so much fun. I posed for pictures, chatted to fans and signed loads of books. My mum even stood next to me hugging and chatting to most people haha! It was sooo cute.

I always come away from trips wishing it carried on forever – wishing that I could spend every day with those who watch my videos.

People often ask me if I get tired during meet and greets. I can see why they'd ask as I've done some crazy stints — like eight hour ones before with no breaks — but I never really do.

The reason is because everyone I meet is always so excited, happy and upbeat, which keeps my energy so high, making me excited and chatty. It's like hanging out with tons of friends at once; it's so lovely. New York was seriously amazing and it was even better being able to fly my mum out and have her experience everything with me!

SCAN HERE

BAND AID

One of the craziest things I've been involved with was Band Aid. Like actual Band Aid!

Myself, Zoe and Joe turned up to the recording studio, jumped out of our car to see tons and tons of fans and paparazzi flooding the street. How anyone knew where the recording was taking place I'll never know... but I suppose fans and paps are like detectives, they work out everything!

Whilst doing a few interviews with the press before going inside, everyone started going crazy! I turned my head to see Harry Styles rush past me and run straight inside. Things were about to get real.

All attendees were previously told not to bring any management or security, which confused me because it's not even possible to get close to some of the celebrities who were participating, due to the crazy amount of security around them 24/7.

We walked inside and went straight into the green room where everyone singing on the single was relaxing. It was so surreal. Meeting people you've frequently seen on TV, posters and in music videos in person is weird! It's hard to picture celebrities as real people, but in the green room were some of the most famous people in the world with absolutely no security – just relaxing and chatting to each other.

After chatting to Nick Grimshaw for a while, Zoe, Joe and I grabbed some snacks and sat down at a little round table because we didn't really know many other people. 'Do you want a coffee?' I felt a hand on my shoulder and turned around to say 'no thank you' to see it was Ed Sheeran... Ed was offering to make me a coffee haha!... what was happening?! He sat down at our table and we all spoke about music, YouTube and touring for about 20 minutes before heading into the studio to record the actual track.

I should probably point out that because we're not exactly singers, Zoe, Joe and I were only in the chorus of the song! We were asked to be involved by Bob Geldof who had heard that our videos were popular and decided that he wanted us to be involved to try help raise as much awareness and money for the cause.

Recording the chorus only took about 20 minutes, with everyone huddled up singing away. The entire day was so surreal for so many different reasons.

I feel so lucky and **honoured** to be able to say I've helped an amazing cause with so many talented and inspiring people.

I BELIEVE THERE aRE TWO KiNDS OF FaMiLiES iNTHiS WORLD:

Cat families and dog families.

Growing up I was in a cat family. We've had cats ever since I can remember. Wait! I'm making my family sound weird: we're not like some crazy cat family — we only own two cats! My dad and I always wanted a dog, but I guess since both my parents worked full time, it wouldn't have really been fair to get a dog and then leave it home alone all day whilst Poppy and I were at school and Mum and Dad were at work.

With YouTube being our full-time jobs and enabling us to work from anywhere at anytime, Zoe and I were lucky enough to get a dog!! I sometimes *think having a dog at my age isn't the most normal thing* haha — but I just saw it as my chance to finally get myself a little companion. So after months and months of persuading both my parents (you'll find out why in a minute, keep reading) and Zoe that it was the best idea ever, I managed to breakthrough to them and they agreed!

(I still have no idea how I actually managed to persuade them haha).

My mum planned on cutting down on work by working fewer days per week and it was also coming up to my dad's birthday. So not only were Zoe and I in the position *to get a little puppy*, so were my mum and dad (kinda). They just didn't know they were, haha! I didn't keep my idea as a surprise, because a dog isn't really something they could return if they didn't agree with my 'amazing' birthday present. **Persuading my dad** was easy — all I had to do was ask him and he was sold on the idea! My mum, however, was a little more difficult, but with the help of my dad, we got there in the end.

The breed. A few of my friends have got pugs and if you've ever spent more than one second with a pug, you know what it's like. You walk away wanting one more than anything you've ever wanted before! What's better than one pug? Two pugs haha!! How amazing would it be if Zoe and I were to get a little female pug and my mum and dad were to get her little brother? 'So amazing' is the answer. So that's exactly what we did.

Nala and Buzz.

Nala

Don't get me wrong, I knew looking after and training a puppy would be a big challenge and completely change my life within a second. I was well aware of that from the countless books Zoe and I read up on before the puppy arrived. But words cannot describe how much work a puppy is!!

I thought I was aware... yeah... I wasn't at all.

Imagine having a little baby who runs around ALL day and can't wear a nappy... *that's a puppy:* pooing everywhere and eating everything, haha! Oh and I should also mention *the no sleeping part...* I had to spend every night sleeping next to her; otherwise she wouldn't sleep and would just cry. Yeah, that too.

Having said that, things did get better within a matter of weeks. Each day that passed was easier and easier, but damn, if you **ever think you're** ready for a puppy... you're not. But once you're put in the position and you've purchased your little companion, you have to make yourself ready — that's the only option.

I suppose that's what it must be like when you have children. You're never really 'ready' until the baby's born and then you make yourself ready.

I wouldn't change anything about Nala; she's my little friend. I love her so much! I know people who have dogs often say weird things, like they 'talk' to their dog, or that their dog can tell when they're not having a great day, but trust me it's true.
The bond between me and Nala is the best. I want her with me at all time.

...Unless she's being naughty, which is quite often. She's a crazy little one!

The Pointless Book went down better than I could have ever imagined! **My viewers went crazy** for it, resulting in the book staying at number #1 in the charts for 17 weeks... little did they know I'd been working my butt off on The Pointless Book 2! Filled with similar kinda things, my aim for the sequel was to develop popular pages from the first book and to simply make it better than the first.

The book sold like crazy! I think it did even better than first one did in the first few weeks of its publication, which was mad! And just like with the first book, before I could even blink I had finished my UK book tour and was on a plane to America and Canada.

Touring is intense because the viewers know where I'm going to be every second of the day — they know when I'm at the airport, which hotel I'm staying in, they even work **out which** restaurant I'm eating at!

The crowds are everywhere — it's like a crazy rollercoaster of non-stop meeting people.

As I'm sure I've said at some point throughout this book so far, I love meeting those who watch my videos! There's nothing quite like being able to say thank you for everything in person.

The opportunity to do this with viewers who live literally on the other side of the world is crazy.

I love being on tour and it's so much fun meeting different people across all the cities I visited. It's hard, though, for people watching my videos, because I'm so busy each day that my daily vlogs tend to become kinda similar. So with the America and Canada tour, I made sure I was able to do lots of fun activities in each city I went to.

Toronto

I discovered poutine while walking down Queen Street and I cannot even describe to you how good that stuff is! England NEEDS more poutine. Oh and we also walked on the scary glass floor at the top of the CN Tower.

Atlanta

Maddie (my manager) and I set ourselves the challenge of going to the gym at least every other day, but we kinda failed.

In Atlanta we were staying in a crazy-lovely hotel with an amazing gym. Whilst getting changed to go out, I noticed a spa treatment booklet and if you know me, you know I love a good massage – but I'm yet to find one where I haven't fallen asleep in the first five minutes. Although I think that's a good sign because it means I'm super-relaxed, right?

Anyways, I called up the spa and booked both of us in for full body massages under the condition that we go to the gym at least once, haha.
Maddie and I ~~have~~ have an ongoing joke about something weird that ALWAYS happens to me when I get a massage.

If you've never experienced getting a professional massage before, they usually light candles around the room and put a warm flannel on your face before they start the actual massage. Well except with me. And again, I have no idea why this always happens to me... but it does and Maddie LOVES to laugh about it.

So we both go off into separate rooms with our masseurs and the man massaging me doesn't just put the flannel on my face... but begins to rub my legs and feet with it... **literally like he is washing me!** I had a shower before going down to the spa to receive the massage, so it's not **like I was dirty or anything!**

The massage finishes and I walk into the little **waiting room where Maddie's** waiting for me and I ask if her masseur **used a flannel.** She looks really confused and says she doesn't believe me. I told her it happened again _ the whole flannel thing! (I think this story is the kinda one where you have to be there for it to be funny, but trust me we ~~while~~ were dying with laughter). So now, **every time a massage is mentioned,** Maddie laughs and says something like 'it's time for your wash!' We **also went on**

a **Segway** tour, which was so much fun! I'd never been on one before and came off of the 2.5 hour tour wanting to buy one so so bad...

until I realised they're like **£6,000,** or something crazy. They're the best thing ever for lazy people like me, haha!

Boston

Harvard University was a million times more impressive than I had ever imagined it to be. I know I never went to uni, but I swear it was the most typical American movie-looking uni I've ever seen! If I did go to uni, I would have loved to go to Harvard. Not just because it's Harvard haha, but because the architecture and grounds were so beautiful.

New York

Poppy's birthday was during my time in New York so I thought it would be amazing to fly her and Sean (her boyfriend) out to spend some time with us.

I booked them flights that landed a few days before I arrived in the city and into the same hotel as me, and then we all flew back a few days later, making their stay just over a week.

Neither of them had been to New York before and I knew they were going to be obsessed! Every day Poppy would call me to tell me about all the exciting things they were getting up to and all the food they were eating, haha. I landed in New York and went straight to their hotel room to say hello! It was so crazy seeing my sister on the other side of the world. We had so much fun, including going to a super-fun Japanese restaurant where they cooked all the food in front of you at your table. Oh and don't let me forget the meal out with Joey Graceffa too; I love that boy!

Basically I had the best 10 days ever. I met thousands and thousands of people who watched my videos, travelled throughout America and did some amazingly fun things with such good friends and family!

Growing up I never even imagined I'd be able to visit America before being a proper adult (being 22 doesn't count, I still feel like I'm 18). YouTube has allowed me to do the most crazy things!

A day doesn't pass by where I don't sit and think about how lucky I am to be able to do this and call it my job.

My good friend Jim Chapman had recently become engaged to his soon-to-be-wife Tanya Burr and do you know what that meant?

STAG DO!

Around eight of us jumped on a plane to France for a snowboarding trip for a few days. I should point out how incredibly hard it is to get that many YouTubers together at the SAME time. I can't even begin to tell you how many crap jokes were made by Leon on that trip... don't ever listen to anything that comes out that guy's mouth haha!

In fact, most of the words that came out of any of our mouths during the trip were either rubbish insults at each other, or daring each other to do stupid things, such as walk the entire way home naked... yeah I'll ~~leave~~ leave you to work out who that was!

Don't get me wrong, the snowboarding was awesome,

I even ended up buying a snowboard on the last day. Yeah I know, kinda stupid to buy one on the LAST day. Nice one Alfie. The best part was just hanging out with the guys and the opportunity to spend proper quality time all together. Yeah we see each other at events and meetings, but it's not the same as when all the boys are together.

Out on the snow we messed about so much – daring each other to try stupid tricks and jumps where 99% of the time we ended up with our butts slamming on the ice.

Caspar was the funniest: **he literally doesn't care at all** and goes for **anything you tell** him to, which he somehow manages to pull off (and it's sick!)! He's even better than Marcus, who likes to think of himself as a **pro hahahaha!**

Wait how did I nearly forget about Leon crashing a wedding in a bar we were in **and spending the entire evening dancing with them?! Leon's hips are like no other.** As soon as he hears a song he likes there's no stopping him! He's an animal on the dance floor and let's just say I felt **sorry for the bride and** groom because he KILLED it with every move you can imagine.

Jimbo if you're reading this, **thanks for such** an amazing **time and congratulations again to you and Tan** x

SCAN HERE

IT's CRAZY HOW YOUR LiFE CAN FLASH BEFORE YOUR VERY EYES.

I remember being 11 years old and wishing I was 16 so I could stay up later in the evenings and do the fun things teenagers can do. Now here I am at 22 not knowing where the time has gone! Don't wish anything away; enjoy every moment you have!

It's absolutely mad to think that I've now been doing YouTube for six years... what even?! Where has the time gone? It feels like yesterday that I put my family

camera on a little stack of books and DVDs in my bedroom and filmed my first video. It feels like yesterday that I hit 100 subscribers, 1,000 subscribers and now somehow 4,000,000 subscribers.

There aren't many negatives about making videos for YouTube as a full-time job. Well actually that's not true! There is one thing that sometimes does get a little tricky and that's being able to stop 'working'. ~~When~~ I love what I do so damn much; I want to create videos all day every day and when other things get in the way, such as dentist appointments etc, I don't want to go to them haha!

I find it really hard to sleep at night. My head's buzzing with different video ideas and I just want to jump up and go film/edit. To be honest I kinda wish humans didn't have to sleep so I could get more done each day.

Separating 'work' and 'non-work' time is so hard when you love what you do, so I decided to create a fun and inspiring area where **I could to go and 'work' each day, which will help me create** even better content. I searched online for months and months until I found the perfect office not too far from my house. The feel and look is like nothing I've seen in Brighton before. **The** shape and style is sooo me, I became obsessed and had to rent it even if it was much bigger than I needed.

I'm not too great at planning or waiting **for things.**

I'm used to filming a video, editing and uploading it within a day or two, so anything that takes longer than a few days really bugs me. **Poppy's so, so good at planning,** organising and designing things, that was literally her job after uni, designing an art studio and planning where each piece of art goes etc. We sat down on the floor in my new office with pen, **paper and a tape measure and** planned out what we needed and what was going to go where.

We smashed it in one day.

I've been asked a few times why I need an office if I'm just filming videos. But what people don't realise is how nice it can be to leave an office and **to actually go home.**

There are tons of meetings and boring bits I have to do — **it's not all just creating fun videos** (even though it looks like that), so being able to ~~to be~~ leave the meetings behind and arrive home where no work, or only fun work happens, is super-nice. *But it's more* *than that: as you know I love buying weird* *gadgets and toys, so being able to build an office* with a table tennis table and other cool things inspires me and keeps my videos fun and stupid like they've always been since day one.

It's also nice having somewhere dedicated to filming. Before, **when I wanted to film a** **sit-down vlog or challenge, I'd have to tidy** **up our bedroom and make it look all nice to film** **in;** now I've got somewhere that is only used for filming, which is so much more efficient and allows me to film more regularly (and doesn't **disturb Zoe or Nala!**).

So many exciting projects have months and months of work that go into them before anyone can even know that they're going on and an amazing example of this is our Zalfie wax figures at Madame Tussauds London!

When leaving Madame Tussauds, you're asked for your most wished-for celebrity waxwork and somehow Zoe and I were the most-requested people in 2015?!
Crazy I know, don't ask me how or why, I don't understand it!

We received an email asking us if we'd like to be put into the wax museum, which only adds a couple of new people each year. My initial response was like what? how? why? when? huh? What's going on? I can't go in Madame Tussauds...I just make little YouTube videos; I'm not a celebrity!

But once the Madame Tussauds team explained that it's literally done on whoever is the most requested that year, it made me sit back and think about why we were even considering turning this opportunity down! If people were telling Madame Tussauds they wanted us there, why would I say no to that?

Zoe and I spent days and days in different studios doing photoshoots — sat in the strangest of positions for hours on end whilst being spun around. We even took Nala along to some of the shoots to sit with us whilst we were being measured up. At one point I was sat in my boxers for literally 6 hours with some-one measuring every single part of my body, with

tiny stickers stuck all over me to help calculate the distances.

I'm super-fussy about what my hair looks like each day, let alone an entire **wax figure of ME! Each pie**ce of hair is hand-pressed into my wax head and dyed/trimmed to look like mine. Layers and layers of paint and make-up was put on my body and face to match my own skin colour... The work that was put into making my figure was ridiculous!

The big day was here! **Zoe and I** could finally tell our audiences what we'd been working on secretly for so long! Annnd we could also finally see Zoe and I in actual Madame Tussauds in London in our remade bedroom, looking as though we were vlogging!

All of our friends and family came down for the grand opening and it was just crazy to see so much support for such a surreal opportunity.

Each and every day I get so many messages from people sending pictures of 'me' with them, when in fact it's them and my wax figure! I love that they can kinda get to meet me any day of the year, **even when I'm** busy **and at home.**

I feel like I'm going to regret writing this because, knowing me, I'm going to forget something or someone, so I'm sorry if I've forgotten you! Let's take a step back and look at just how many amazing things my friends have all achieved.

I've written a lot a about me, but my close YouTube friends are taking over the world and I'm so, so proud of them!

Marcus: A book. SourcedBox (yum!). Music video and song.

Zoe: Two bestselling books. A product line. 10 million subscribers. A wax figure in Madame Tussauds.

Joe: A bestselling graphic novel. A film.

Connor Franta: A book. A new creative company.

Troye: EP wild. Debut album Blue Neighbourhood.

Louise: A chart-topping book. A diary. A clothing line.

Dan and Phil: A book. App.

Chai: Moved to London and traveled to tons of countries.

Niomi: SourcedBox (yum!).

Tyler: A crazy-good book. A podcast. Merchandise. A tour. A documentary.

Joey: An awesome book. Crazy (and I mean crazy) good shorts (films not actually shorts haha!).

Jim: Stationery line. Merchandise. TV presenting.

Poppy: A blog, which is killing it!!

Tanya: An amazing book. A product line.

Caspar: A film. Merchandise.

...and so so many more!

JUST REALISED I HAVEN'T REALLY WRITTEN ENOUGH ABOUT HOW SUPPORTIVE ALL MY NON-YOUTUBE FRIENDS IN BRIGHTON ARE ABOUT MY YOUTUBE VIDEOS, AND THE FACT THAT I'M BUSY 99% OF THE TIME AND NOT ABLE TO SEE THEM AS OFTEN AS I'D LIKE TO.

Going to get a little deep for a second now: hanging out with people who don't create YouTube videos can often be a little bit tricky because they want to know so much about what I'm up to and how it's all going, that sometimes it feels like I'm being interviewed. I know for sure they don't mean it; they're just interested to know how I've been and what I've been doing. But it can often be a little intense, and as odd as it sounds, as I make videos about my life every day... I don't actually really like to talk about myself. So I find it weird when friends spend the time we have together talking about me. I often have to work really hard to move the conversation away from myself and onto other topics.

But my friends from back at school – you guys know who you are, are always so amazing and ignore all the YouTube stuff and just chill and have fun whilst we're hanging out!

I THOUGHT I was GOING TO DIE

The crazy thing about making friends with people online is that you can know them so well from tweeting/texting and watching their videos, but you may not have actually met them in real life.

This is exactly what happened with me, Roman and Britt: we'd chatted online for ages, but since they live in America and I live in the UK it was nearly impossible for us to spend time together.

We got DM'ing late one night on Twitter to see if we were all free to hang out. Bear in mind that messaging each other was a little ~~difficult~~ difficut due to the time difference.

I woke up with a message from Roman saying he was free over the next week... no notice – literally the week we were **texting haha! And somehow, by chance, so was I!**

I love to be spontaneous, but I've never done something quite like what I did next. I went online there and then and booked flights for the next morning super-early and then messaged him to say **I'm coming to stay for the next 5 days haha!** I kinda even forgot to tell my friends. Zoe knew, of course, because she was going to have to look after Nala and I think I also told my family, but before I knew it I was at the airport.

Five minutes later I received a call from my manager asking me if I was around the next day for a meeting

and I suddenly realised I hadn't even told my management I was going! I had quite a ~~few~~ few meetings in my diary for that week (including writing this book!) so kinda had to break the news that I was about to fly to America...and was already in the airport haha.

I'd never flown alone before, but I like time to myself so I thought, if anything, I'd enjoy it and just relax. After a quick change-over in Chicago, I hopped on the smallest plane I've ever seen in my life... honestly I thought I wasn't going to make it.

First of all the plane was the size of a tiny private jet, minus the luxury insides haha! I think there were 7 or 12 people on the flight and we were ALL sitting right near the front... now me being super-observant of everything ever, I clocked onto this straight away and just assumed more passengers must be coming on any second. Welllllllll... that was until the one air hostess on board closed the tiny little plane door and noted on a piece of tissue that we were all there.

A PIECE OF TISSUE. Not even paper!

She looked a little confused and then told us that the plane might be flying with its nose pointing down, which is why we were all at the front.

I WANTED TO GET OFF *OF THE PLANE.*

I honestly felt like it wasn't even worth the risk! Why was I on this? **Was Roman pranking me?** I spent most of the flight listening to a calming app on my phone **with my head in my hands.**

A plane journey has never gone so slowly in my life. It was meant to be 1 hour and 30 minutes, but for some reason and don't even ask me why, it only took 50 minutes! Maybe all the weight at the front made us fly faster hahaha.

Arriving at the airport to see viewers waiting for me was so refreshing! I could ~~speak~~ speak to people about my weird near-death experience.

Walking outside I could see Roman and Britt's MASSIVE (and I mean MASSIVE) red pick-up style truck. I hopped in and it was like we'd known each for years! Well I guess we did, but had just never met before.

Spending a few days in a completely different environment, laughing at all the differences we had and trying new things, was crazy. It's not often I get to travel without meetings, book signings **or YouTube meet** ups. Saying that, we kept ourselves busy. I swear we did more in those few days than I usually do in a month! But more importantly I came away with two amazing new friends who I know will be staying with me in the UK some time soon and that excites me so much.

I came away feeling so refreshed and inspired to create better videos than ever before. Both Roman and Britt's love of vlogging is like nothing I've ever seen.

They're both so engaged with their audience and spend all day, every day making sure their videos are as fun and entertaining as possible. Honestly it made me sit back and reminded me why I'm doing YouTube and showed me why I love it so damn much.

Big thanks to Roman and Britt for making my stay so much fun and for welcoming me into their home. Oh and don't let me forget Kane the master of the Lego game, with whom I we spent hours playing on the Playstation haha!

Keeping motivated in life is one of the most important things. If you don't love what you do, you need to do everything to change that. No one should accept working a job they don't enjoy. I'm not saying quit your job and play video games every day and expect it to become your job. But what I mean is: spend ALL your spare time working your butt off on doing what you LOVE. What's the worst that can happen? You finish work at 5pm, but you can spend all your spare time enjoying yourself. And the best? The best that can happen is when your passion, your hobby, your dream job becomes reality, and all of your hard work outside of work has enabled you to gradually finish the original job you disliked and you can now focus on what you LOVE.

This is one of my favourite quotes of all time:

'If you don't build your own dream, someone else will hire you to help build theirs.'
– Tony Gaskins

Annd this pretty much brings me up to today January 20th 2016. I'm currently sat in my office spending most of my days in meetings, filming/editing videos and planning new, exciting projects.

This year is purely about videos. I want to put 99% of my time and effort into creating the best videos I possibly can. It's far too easy to be carried away by the amazing opportunities, but I always like to remind myself of the most important thing in every situation and if my videos drop in quality, then those opportunities won't be available any longer.

Last year I often left filming videos to the very last minute. I'd end up filming/editing and uploading all in one day, which resulted in a few rushed videos, me being really stressed and meant I had tons of issues with my chest. Don't worry the pains are sorted now!

So yeah, this year I'm planning all my videos way in advance (as much as possible haha!) and I'm going to be so on top of all my work! So far 2016 is going very well. I've got so many exciting things planned and I can't wait for my audience to hear about them!

2016 IS going to be the best year of my life so far.

I WANT TO TRAVEL THE WORLD.

All my college friends took gap years to go to places such as Thailand, Vietnam, Australia and China, but because I was busy working on YouTube stuff, I never got the chance to properly travel. Don't get me wrong, I've seen a lot of the world – via different YouTube events, book signings, **meet ups** – but I haven't done any backpacking or any REAL travelling where I'm not sat in a hotel 90% of the time.

This year I want to pack a big bag full of camera equipment and go travelling! Whether that means planning an awesome adventure with friends or even going to the airport with a friend and buying a ticket for the next available flight (and not knowing where we're going until the last minute or how we're even going to get home!). The thought of that excites me so much and I really want to make it happen!

'ALFIE YOU'RE 22 AND YOU HAVEN'T GOT A DRIVER'S LICENCE... COME ON!'

...is what everyone around me is saying, haha! I WILL pass my driving test this year.

I will. I will. I will.

As I'm sure you've gathered by now, putting my life online is literally my life. I wake up every day looking forward to creating videos and talking to those who watch them.
However this year I think it'll be important for me to have the odd week offline every now and again for holidays with my family, or visiting friends who don't make YouTube videos. I had my first proper break, a week off at the end of 2015 and it was so crazy! Not filming my life was so surreal: at first I didn't enjoy not filming, then after three days I felt so relaxed about not having to worry about having the time to edit and upload, or if the internet is even going to be good enough to upload.

There's so much that goes into daily vlogging and I often feel that the viewers see the 15 minute video and forget how much time/effort goes into those videos seven days a week, 365 days a year... Let alone making another eight videos a week on top of that, like I do! But yeah, this year I think I'm going to try have a few days offline every now and again just to make sure I'm living in the moment and fully enjoy everything I'm doing in life.

THANK YOU!

I've never once thrown away a letter or card that a viewer has given me. They're stored in boxes and boxes and boxes in my parents' house, my house and even my office, and this year I'd love to take some time out to sit down and read through them. There's such an overwhelming amount that I don't think it'd even be possible to read them all in a year, haha! I'll probably read a few each day until I'm like 80 or something. Reading them can be my little pick-me-up each morning. Some people need their morning coffee to get them up and ready for the day haha, but I'll be reading my 'fan' mail to get me up and ready!

Seriously though, I appreciate all the time and effort that everyone has put into the cards and letters, and for sure I will read them all at some point don't you worry!

This also ties in with press work. I've done so many amazing photoshoots and interviews, but often don't get time to actually take in how crazy it all is. Luckily my mum tries to purchase everything I'm in and is turning it all into a scrapbook for me to look back on. So maybe starting this year, or next year, I'll start reading through it all and reflect on all the amazing things I'm lucky enough to be able to have done so far on this journey.

I can't even begin to describe how fortunate and lucky I feel to have done so many amazing things at the age of 22 **and it's only because of YOU** reading this. You've honestly **made my dreams** come true... wait, not even my dreams. I would never have even dreamt about some of the things that have happened to me!

I have so much to thank **my family for! They've** always ways been so, so incredibly supportive and are always there if I ever need advice, or help with anything and for sure this doesn't go unnoticed! **Mum, Dad** and Pop you guys are the best family I could have asked **for!**

What I've managed to achieve is something you could easily do yourself. *You reading this could easily be in my position experiencing the same things* I have and I don't want you to forget that. I'm not anything special.

I'm just a normal person **who's had some not-so-normal things** happen in my life so far. Don't EVER let anyone tell you **that you're not good enough.** Spend every hour of every day proving to them that you are!

Never settle for less than you deserve!

221

I don't know where my future is going to lead me, but what I do know is that I'd love for you to carry on this journey with me as I know it's going to be a fun one! We've ~~always~~ achieved so much together so far and I honestly believe that it's only just begun. I'm only 22 so there's a lot more to experience and go through together. Let's plan some amazing and crazy stuff and hopefully I'll even get to meet you in person along the way.

I've spent so many hours in bed, in my office, on the sofa, on trains... literally anywhere I could writing this scrapbook and I don't know whether to be sad that it's coming to an end or happy that I've enjoyed looking back on everything so much.

This book is a piece of me. Each page freezes a moment of my life in time. I hope you've found the weird little stories from throughout my life interesting... and if you didn't then at least I will when I look back at it in years to come haha!

Alfie xx

22nd January 2016

PS - I passed my driving test 1st time, didn't I!